FAULKNER'S
OXFORD

FAULKNER'S OXFORD
Recollections and Reflections

Herman E. Taylor

Rutledge Hill Press
Nashville, Tennessee

PS
3511
.A86
Z7948
1990

Published in Nashville, Tennessee, by Rutledge Hill Press, Inc. 513 Third Avenue South, Nashville, Tennessee 37210 Typography by Bailey Typography, Nashville, Tennessee

Library of Congress Cataloging-in-Publicatin Data

Taylor, Herman E.
    Faulkner's Oxford : recollections and reflections / Herman E. Taylor.
        p. cm.
    Includes bibliographical references.
    ISBN 1-55853-086-X
    1. Faulkner, William, 1897–1962—Homes and haunts—Mississipppi—Oxford. 2. Novelists, American—20th century—Biography.
    3. Taylor, Herman E.—Friends and associates. 4. Oxford (Miss.) in literature. 5. Oxford (Miss.)—Biography. I. Title
    PS3511.A86Z7948 1990
    813'.52—dc20   90-48932
    [B]   CIP

            1 2 3 4 5 6 7 — 96 95 94 93 92 91 90
            Manufactured in the United States of America

Faulkner's Oxford is dedicated to the author's beloved wife, Nina Claire. Without her encouragement and assistance this book would never have been written.

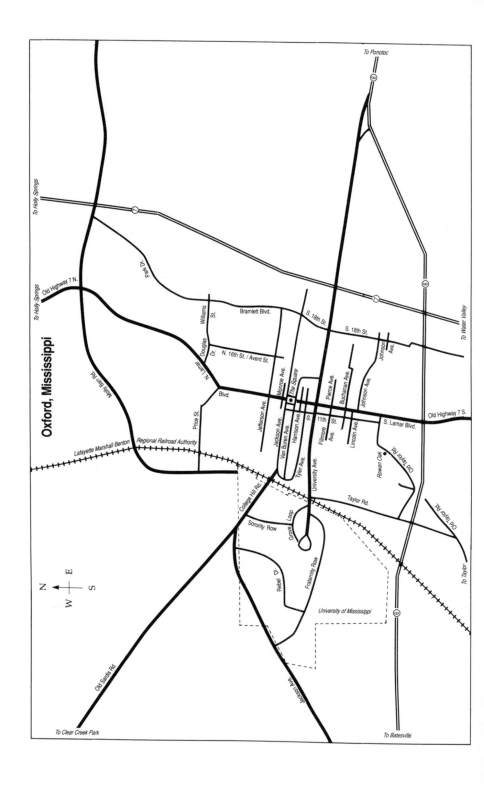

Foreword

Faulkner's Oxford is a recollection and reminiscense of the people, places, and events which may have inspired some of the writings and influenced the life of William Faulkner. I first encountered William Faulkner when I was five years old, in 1924, and I followed his career as a writer until he died in 1962.

This book describes some aspects of Faulkner's life which were revealed to me in my personal acquaintance with "Mr. Billy" and other members of the Falkner family.

Much of William Faulkner's writings dealt with Yoknapatawpha County and the town of Jefferson, which, of course, were fictional names for Mississippi's Lafayette County and the city of Oxford. Some similarities appear to have existed between my ancestors and those of William Faulkner. Such similarities may be typical of many families of the early settlers of Mississippi and thus seem worth mentioning.

Captain Daniel Taylor (1748-1826), my great-great-great-grandfather, served in the Continental Army from North Carolina. He later settled in the Mississippi Territory in what later became Carroll County, where he died in 1826. He was the father of Dr. John Taylor who came to the vicinity of Taylor, Mississippi, in the Chickasaw Indian Territory around 1810 in what would later become Lafayette County, Mississippi.

Colonel William Clark Falkner (1825-1889) was the great-grandfather of William Cuthbert Faulkner, the renowned and Nobel Prize-winning author. Colonel Falkner served the Confederate cause during the Civil War and commanded the Second Mississippi Infantry Regiment for a time. He had come to Mississippi around 1828 and had settled in northwest Mississippi in what became the town of Falkner in Tippah County.

Beginning with Dr. John Taylor and Colonel William Clark Falkner, the Falkner and Taylor descendants have shared in the history and environment of Mississippi for seven generations. Some lived in the Mississippi Territory before it became a state and before the Indians were dispossessed and before the creation of Lafayette County in 1836. The town of Falkner, Mississippi, is a few miles north of Ripley, Mississippi. The town of Taylor, Mississippi, is in Lafayette County, a few miles south of Oxford, Mississippi.

William Cuthbert Faulkner's great-grandfather, William Clark Falkner, is said to have engaged in the building of a railroad in North Mississippi. My great-great-grandfather, Dr. John Taylor, founded the town of Taylor, Mississippi, and is said to have built the first water-powered mill in Lafayette County. The mill, reportedly, was on the Yocona River near Taylor, Mississippi.

Members of both of these families served in the Confederate Army during the Civil War, and they have lived in Lafayette County for more than a century.

Recent generations of both of these families have lived in Oxford and have remained friends and sometimes neighbors and have touched each other's lives in countless instances. This book is based upon my personal recollection of Mr. Billy and reflections upon his writings.

—Herman E. Taylor

Table of Contents

Foreword

FAULKNER'S
OXFORD

Recollections

Chapter 1

Rendezvous

On a bright, sunny summer morning in 1924 in Oxford, Mississippi, I was returning home from an errand I had run for my mother. No intuition hinted to me that the adventures of that day would be worth remembering or writing about.

My mother had sent me "up town" to mail a letter for her. As Oxford had no home mail delivery in those days, most people in the town found it necessary to go to the post office on the northeast corner of the square each day to pick up their mail at the General Delivery window or from their rented mail box.

If I lingered on the post office steps, there was a good chance that I would, in the course of a day, see most of the people of Oxford. Thus the trek to the post office became an important matter and provided an opportunity for meeting and socializing and keeping up with what was going on and exchanging bits of gossip.

Often I had accompanied my mother when she mailed her reports and orders to the Realsilk Hosiery Company that she represented as a salesperson. There was scarcely a street in Oxford that we had not walked in the course of her business calls, and I knew the occupants of almost every house in town. At that time Oxford had a population of about twenty-five hundred, plus another few hundred faculty members and students who resided on the campus of the University of Mississippi which lay to the west of town.

After the letter was mailed that summer morning, I walked down the steps and stopped momentarily to look at a U.S. Army recruiting poster which showed a picture of a soldier holding a Springfield rifle and attired in what I recognized as a World War I steel helmet and uniform. Then the prevailing westerly wind brought me the scent of roasting coffee beans from McElroy's Grocery Store, on the north side of the square. The smell was so good that I turned and walked along the north sidewalk past Brown's general store. Isaac Brown and his son Willie operated this store where most things needed by farmers could be purchased, from groceries to plow lines, horse collars, overalls, and hardware.

When I reached the corner of North Street, I cut a diagonal course across the square to the courtyard which surrounded the Lafayette County Courthouse, which was the center of political, legal, and business activities in Lafayette County. Already the benches in the courtyard had begun to fill with the elderly men who met there daily to talk of politics and crops and the morning news as brought to them by the Memphis *Commercial Appeal,* the daily morning newspaper. I had heard it said that the people in North Mississippi believed in the Bible, Sears and Roebuck catalogues, and the *Commercial Appeal.*

As I opened the courthouse door, I sensed the unpleasant smell of disinfectant which had drifted upwards from the public toilet in the basement of the old building. Other smells struck my nostrils and I discerned that these were from the three spittoons in the center of the hallway. Tobacco chewers and snuff-dippers spat at or near the spittoons, missing as often as hitting their intended target. During cold or rainy weather I had seen considerable numbers of country folk sitting or squatting on the floor of the hallway, talking politics or business or merely passing the time of day. The floors had been covered with some oily substance such as linseed oil or "dustdown," and it too added to the amalgamation of the courthouse smells.

On the first floor were the offices of the circuit clerk, the chancery clerk, the tax assessor, and the sheriff. There was also an open space, perhaps thirty feet wide, from which a flight of stairs led upward to the courtroom for the circuit and chancery courts. In the high-ceilinged courtroom within my recollection, there were always tattered window shades at the tall and narrow windows.

From the courtroom I could walk north or south onto the second floor porches, which were built above the arched concrete entrances. The porches were surrounded by an iron railing between the four great columns which rose from the porch floors to support the arched roof. Atop the building was the town clock with large faces toward the north, south, east, and west, which could be seen from most parts of Oxford and the surrounding areas. The clock tower rose many feet above the highest part of the courthouse roof and was covered with copper which had weathered to a blackish appearance.

In the southwest corner of the first floor was the office of the sheriff and tax collector. The sheriff's office was especially interesting to me. Here it was that everyone suspected or accused of crime was brought to be questioned and "booked" before being led off to the county jail, a block to the north on North Street, or set free.

Only rarely did I ever see the sheriff in that office. Much of the time he was out and about the town and county in which he was the chief law enforcement officer. He had about nine hundred square miles of Lafayette County to patrol.

Also sharing the sheriff's office was the justice of the peace for the civil district. The justice handled much judicial business from his chair near the south window of the sheriff's office. This was where everyone accused of drunkenness, gambling, whoring, disturbing the peace, or bootlegging would begin to answer to "the law."

As I left the courthouse, passing underneath the great concrete entranceway, I descended the two steps from the courthouse entrance to the walkway which led to the south entrance of the courtyard. The courtyard was surrounded by a wrought-iron fence, providing a convenient place to hitch horses and mules. In the early 1920s most people still traveled by horse-drawn carriages and wagons although automobiles and trucks were becoming more common on the streets of Oxford.

A small flock of pigeons was walking around on the little patch of grass between the barren ground and the sidewalk. The grass had been worn away by people walking diagonally from one courtyard entrance to another. The pigeons, with a noisy flapping of wings, suddenly took flight as I walked down the walkway to the south.

A large oak tree stood on each side of the south walkway, each about fifteen feet from the walk. I shuddered slightly and avoided looking directly at the tree on the west side of the walk because I had been told that in 1908 a man had been lynched for a murder and had been hanged from a limb of that tree. I always felt that there was shame upon that tree.

When I reached the entrance to the courtyard, I stepped down a couple of steps to the level at which the Confederate Monument stood. It had been erected by the United Daughters of the Confederacy around 1907 in honor of the men from Lafayette County who had served the Confederate cause in the Civil War. Atop the shaft there was a statue of a soldier with a gun resting near his feet as he faced to the south down South Street.

After I passed the monument I stopped on the step which led down to the graveled surface of the square. A wagon heavily loaded with watermelons and cantaloupes and pulled by two mules was turning across my intended path. I guessed that it was heading for the northwest corner of the courtyard where it would be parked along the fence and remain there until the melons were sold, since this was the usual place where farm products were brought for sale.

The driver wore faded overalls and a light blue shirt and had heavy field shoes on his feet and a wide-brimmed straw hat on his head. As the wagon entered the square, it turned to the left and crossed between me and Rowland's Drug Store, which was on the corner of South Street where it joined the square.

Close behind the wagon came a shiny black buggy pulled by a single horse. The driver was a man of fifty or sixty years, who had steel gray hair where it showed beneath his broad-brimmed Panama hat. He was well dressed, wearing a navy blue suit and white shirt, and at his collar was a neatly tied string bow tie. He wore well-shined black shoes and his black socks were tight around his

The Lafayette County Courthouse in 1908
This photograph was taken from the location of the First National Bank of Oxford, where William Faulkner's grandfather, John Wesley Thompson Falkner, once served as president. During the 1920s and 30s, farmers would park their wagons near the wrought iron fence and sell their produce.

ankles as if held in place by supporters. As he turned to the left across the square, I had a feeling that here was an important man, perhaps a judge, or minister, or "gentleman farmer," who had driven into town to attend to some important matter and who, after attending to business, would perhaps walk around the square to be seen and to speak and "politic" with all he chanced to meet.

As I waited to cross the square, I glanced toward the southeast corner of South Street and the square and caught a glimpse of a large bunch of bananas hanging near the window of a grocery store. The stalk was suspended by a rope from the ceiling of the store and rotated slightly so I could discern each banana. Once

19

The Confederate Monument on the Square
The monument near the south entrance to the Lafayette County Courthouse was erected by the United Daughters of the Confederacy in 1907.

when I was in that store, there had been a barrel of sour cucumber pickles on the floor beneath the spot where the bananas were hanging. I had bought a large pickle and some crackers for a nickel.

I was about to cross the square when I noticed a large black, glistening automobile approaching the square from South Street. The car was so shiny it appeared to have been recently polished. Here and there some shiny metal added emphasis to the care which had been given that car. In the front seat was a Negro chauffeur who wore a cap with a bill pulled down. In the back seat sat an elderly man with gray hair protruding from beneath his hat. He appeared to be looking from side to front to side so as to absorb all that could be seen along his route. I instantly recognized this man as Mr. J. E. Neilson, the owner of the J. E. Neilson Company, a department store which was almost as old as Oxford itself. Mr. Neilson lived on South Street only a block from my mother's home and I had passed his house almost every day. When his car reached the square, it turned to the east and glided over to the front of his store. The chauffeur got out and opened the car door for Mr. Neilson. Mr. Neilson alighted and stepped up the high step to the sidewalk, then stopped to greet and chat with several passersby before going inside the store.

At this point, I was suddenly aware of a new and different sound that I had not heard before on the square. It was that of a high-pitched horn that I had heard before on some Model-T Ford cars and trucks. I looked in the direction of the sound. From the north-west side of the square, a Ford truck was approaching. It sounded as though the muffler was broken, and it was loaded with freshly sawn two-by-fours, piled so high that it seemed that at any moment they would topple and turn the small truck over on its side. The lumber was fastened with a chain but had shifted slightly so that the top of the lumber was several inches further to the side than was the bottom.

The hood had been removed, probably to help keep the motor from overheating when the truck might be required to do hard pulling, as on a country road or hillside trail where logs were being hauled to a sawmill. This truck appeared to have been hard at work and to have been driven a considerable distance in coming into Oxford because its wheels were covered with mud around the rims.

The driver was a man of about twenty. The old hunting cap which he wore was covered heavily with dust. He wore an old denim jumper, a sort of coat which was often worn with overalls, and a red workshirt underneath the jumper. Sweat was running down his face in the midmorning sun. From the corner of his mouth protruded a "roll-your-own" cigarette butt. Whether from a feeling that he needed to warn those who might be in his path of progress, or merely from a desire to announce that he had made it into town with his heavy load, he blew the horn, not at all embarrassed when everyone within the sound looked his way.

He drove around the square until he reached South Street,

where he turned south and proceeded to University Avenue where he turned west. About a mile out University Avenue and about a quarter-mile to the south of the University Bridge over the Illinois Central Railroad was a planing mill, where roughly sawn lumber was planed to exact sizes, then loaded on freight trains for shipment to distant points.

Now the way was clear for me to walk the hundred feet or so across to Rowland's Drug Store.

This was a familiar corner, and the drug store was a place of fascination to me. Once I had gone in the drug store to the fountain where the "soda jerk" made delicious-looking dishes of ice cream, sundaes and banana splits. Those things were far beyond my ability to purchase, but I had had a nickel and I went to the fountain and ordered a "nickel fountain coke." I had sat down at a little round table in a round-bottomed Coca-Cola chair made with twisted wrought-iron legs and back. I had glanced at the magazine rack and saw several magazines that had interesting pictures on their covers. Since I could not read I was unable to tell the names of the magazines, but the thought of growing up and learning to read became a part of my ambition. I looked forward to going to school in September.

On this particular day I had no nickel so I passed along the open door of the drug store and inhaled the odor of some concoction being prepared inside. I always wondered just what it was that made a drug store smell so different from other stores.

As the smells of the drug store fell behind me, I caught the scent of Crowe's Meat Market, which was situated just south of the drug store. Mr. Crowe lived next door to us and a time or two I had been sent to his store to buy some meat when unexpected company arrived at home.

Across the street was Hickey's Blacksmith Shop, and I could smell the smoke from the forge, but this smell was intermingled with an unusually pleasant new-mown grassy smell which came to me from the south. The lawn of the Cumberland Presbyterian Church was being cut by a Negro man with a push lawn mower.

After watching the grass-mowing for a while, I crossed the street to the east side of South Street to see what might be going on there.

With eyes closed and mind elsewhere, I could tell my exact location. The smell of Peacock's Shoe Repair Shop, Mize's Grocery Store, Hickey's Blacksmith Shop, Fudge's Poultry Store, Holley's Ford Garage, or Varner's Repair Shop would tell me where I was.

Hickey's Blacksmith Shop was a source of endless wonderment to me. Andy Hickey lived next door to me and had always been something of a father figure. My own father had died of pneumonia in 1920 when I was a little over a year old, leaving my mother with the formidable problems of rearing five children.

In the blacksmith shop, Mr. Hickey would crank the bellows until the coals in the forge grew red. Then he would thrust a U-shaped piece of iron into the coals. When the iron was red hot, he would take it out and beat on it with his heavy hammer, causing sparks to fly as he shaped it to the hoof of the horse he was shoeing. Then he would take a chisel and cut off whatever was necessary of the two ends of the shoe for it to be the right length. The remaining ends of each leg of the U-shaped iron were beaten into a ninety-degree angle which would give the horse a better footing. Sometimes I would pick up the slugs of iron and carry them with me figuring that they might be fun to shoot in my slingshot instead of the usual rocks.

After the horseshoe had been heated, cut, and bent, Mr. Hickey would plunge it into a half barrel of water. A hissing and whooshing sound would result, and a cloud of steam would shoot towards the ceiling of the shop.

The nervous horse or mule, securely tied and held by a helper, would then be coaxed into raising one foot so that the bottom of his hoof would be exposed. Mr. Hickey would take a sharp knife and cut, trim, and pare the hoof until it was flat enough to firmly seat the new shoe of iron. If the shoe were too long or wide, he would put it back into the forge and heat it red hot again, repeating the process until it was just right.

Next he would take some rectangular-headed nails which sloped from the head down to a sharp point and drive the nail into the hoof. If the point of the nail extended through the hoof, he would snip off the end so that it would be flush with the outside surface of the hoof. This did not hurt the horse. The process would be repeated on each of the horse's hooves until it had a completely new set of shoes and would be able to walk a dirt or graveled road, pull a wagon, plow, or carry his master wherever he might need to go.

Horseshoeing was not all that the blacksmith did. Wagon wheels were made of wood. In order to insure a longer life for them, an iron rim had to be fitted to the outside of each wheel. Other work in the blacksmith shop involved the sharpening of picks, axes, and crosscut saws, and putting new handles on hoes and shovels, and the repairing of the many tools that are necessary in a farming community. There was scarcely any village or hamlet in Mississippi at that time which did not have a blacksmith shop in it. However, sometimes a farmer in a remote area would do his own blacksmithing. My cousin Sam Ragland had a small blacksmith shop, complete with a forge, anvil, and a stone grinding wheel. Standing beneath a large oak tree, he would do such work as was required on his farm, for it would have taken a day's travel to go to the blacksmith's shop in Oxford.

After watching Mr. Hickey at work, I strolled on down the street. Varner's Repair Shop, a block to the south of Hickey's Blacksmith Shop, was equally fascinating to me. Almost every kind of gun, machinery, and equipment was taken there for repair. Mr. Varner, like Mr. Hickey, was a master of his many crafts. I never tired of watching him work. He would undertake the challenge of repairing almost anything. He could replace a refrigerator compressor or motor or do whatever might be necessary to repair any other kind of equipment. He was also a locksmith and could open most any lock when the key had been lost.

Guns and pistols of many kinds were in the racks in the shop along with bicycles and typewriters and locks and keys, but all else faded from my interest as I examined the collection of guns. Looking at and touching shotguns, rifles, and pistols was an experience which captured my imagination. Sometimes I was even able to watch Mr. Varner take the weapon apart and replace a firing pin or clean or oil a pistol.

He had a drill press, a vise, and a metal lathe and could even make parts for some equipment. It seemed that he had a nut or bolt or screw for almost any need.

I had an almost irresistible impulse when passing Mr. Varner's Repair Shop to go in just to see what he might be doing. The shop had a pleasant smell of gun oil and grease and grindstone dust. Some old bicycles which he had rebuilt caused me to fantasize about owning such a bicycle when I grew up.

After having watched Mr. Varner work many times, I had made a shop for myself on my own back porch. I began to assemble all of the tools my mother had and the tool box which my father had used before his death. I built a work bench and began to try to fix things which were broken, like the cord to an electric iron. I sharpened hoes and grass blades and disassembled old clocks and a rifle that my oldest brother had used when he was younger. I imagined that I was doing what Mr. Varner did in his shop.

Curiosity had led me inside Holley's Ford Garage, next door to Varner's Repair Shop, a few times. It seemed almost a miracle how Mr. Mike Williams, the chief mechanic, could take a Model-T Ford engine apart, put it back together again, and make it run. Sometimes I would go around to the back of the garage and pick up some discarded automobile part and examine it to try to figure just how it was made and what it had to do with the running of the vehicle.

In front of Holley's Garage, a genial Negro named Buss, usually dressed in clean coveralls and wearing an official-looking cap with the name of the gasoline which he sold on it, stood awaiting the arrival of a customer. When the customer arrived and asked Buss for five gallons of gas, Buss would pump a hand lever until five gallons showed as being in the glass container at the top of the pump. Then he would put the hose in the gas tank and drain the gas into the car, then take the customer's money inside to the cashier in the office.

Like the businesses around the square, each house along South

Photo courtesy of Jack Cofield

The Cumberland Presbyterian Church
Located one block south of the square, this church was built in the late 1850s, and was used during the Civil War as an armory for the Confederate units of Oxford. By 1940, church membership had dwindled and the church was demolished. Faulkner wrote that while the church had survived when most of the buildings near the square were destroyed by Yankee troops in 1864, it could not withstand the power of commercial interests and the quest for profits from the sale of "toilet paper and bananas."

Street was also a familiar place to me. I walked on past the great gray house of Mrs. Henrietta Goodwin, the first house to the south of the square. She had been a friend of my family for many years. John, her Negro gardener, driver, and general handyman, lived in a small, well-kept, frame house situated at the rear of the larger house and shaded by a mulberry tree. Much of John's time was spent polishing and caring for the glistening Willys-Knight automobile to have it ready for the infrequent, but most important, occasions when Mrs. Goodwin wanted to go for a ride.

Such a household was not unusual in Oxford. What seemed unusual to me was the considerable number of well-to-do, by Oxford standards, women among so many people who were poor or near the poverty level.

Next door, to the south, was the Porter home, a large house of clapboard construction with yellowish peeling paint. There were several of these old houses along South Street, some being rental property and poorly maintained. South Street was the main street running south from the square. The later change of name to South Lamar Boulevard was made to honor Lucius Quintus Cincinnatis Lamar, the town's most illustrious citizen. Lamar was a lawyer and professor who, despite the vindictiveness, suspicions, and prejudices of the post-Civil War period, was able to climb to associate justice of the U.S. Supreme Court. He served in that position from 1888 to 1893. No Mississippian since has reached such judicial height.

Oxford was my native habitat and I was able to spot, if not sense, anything unusual that might be going on. Curiosity and the spirit of adventure made me the "sidewalk superintendent" of every construction project, public or private, and the observer of almost everything out of the ordinary which might occur along the way. These activities might include a farmer-butcher peddling beef from a screened-in meat wagon, or the daily rounds of the Lawhorn ice wagon, which my friends and I followed until someone bought enough ice to cause the ice man to put his hooks into a hundred-pound block, get out his ice-saw, and shower "snow" into waiting hands, to the delight of those who received.

After crossing University Avenue, I passed in front of the J. W. T.

27

Photo courtesy of Jack Cofield

The Young Colonel's Home
This was the home of William Faulkner's grandfather, John Wesley Thompson
Falkner. This was the house that was moved in 1929 to make room on the lot for a
house built for William Faulkner's parents, Murry C. and Maud Falkner.

Falkner home, perhaps the largest house on South Lamar. It was
the home of the grandfather of William, Murry, Jr., Johncy, and
Dean Falkner, and was situated on a lot of about an acre of land
which extended west to Second South Street.

A few years later, the large, three-story, frame house would become the subject of one of the greatest engineering feats I had
ever observed. The house was literally turned ninety degrees to
the north and moved to the edge of the sidewalk on the south side
of University Avenue approximately ten feet from the west property line on the Second South Street side of the lot.

I watched the goings on with near disbelief as the house was
jacked up and placed on log-like rollers. Ropes and pulleys were
used to move the great hulk of the house to its new location where
it would remain for half a century. During those decades it was

used as rental property. Sometimes the apartments were rented to families with several children and a number of my friends would live there.

After the move, it became obvious as to what the motivation might have been. The South Lamar frontage was to be improved with a new brick home for Mr. Murry Falkner, his wife, "Miss Maud," and their sons.

As I continued walking along past the front of the big old Falkner home, about three-fourths of a block south of University Avenue, I spotted something unusual across the street in "Major" Lemuel Early Oldham's yard. I instinctively cut a diagonal course to that side of the street for a closer look.

The Oldham home was another of those large frame houses three stories high. It had a steeply ascending roof with five-feet-wide twin chimneys of reddish bricks. These were near the west

Photo courtesy of Herman E. Taylor

Falkner With A Backward N
The name *Falkner* with the *N* backwards is molded in the concrete of the top step of the walkway that originally led to the home of John Wesley Thompson Falkner. These steps are now in front of the former home of William Faulkner's parents.

The Falkner, Brown, and Gary Home
This house at the corner of South 11th Street and Buchanan Avenue was the Murry Falkner home from 1889 to 1905. William Faulkner lived here during his early childhood. To the rear of the house lies Brown's Pasture.

edge of the roof, nearest South Lamar. They flanked two attic windows which had half circling frames at their tops. A semicircular porch on the front of the house had a roof which was supported by four round columns a foot or so in diameter, contributing to an appearance of architectural elegance in marked contrast to the angular designs of neighboring homes and helping to emphasize the stateliness of the house. From the south side of this porch, a short walkway led to a porte-cochere which was covered with wisteria vines under which the traveler might enter the house.

As I approached the alley, I saw a very large and unusual object. A refrigerator packing box was lying in the front yard! Refrigerators were almost unknown in the homes of Oxford; the ice box on the back porch was the usual place for keeping meat and milk. This was enough to capture my attention, for that yard had always been the epitome of orderliness, presided over by Mrs. Oldham who supervised the work of Prince Wiley. A silent and intense Negro, who was master of his craft, Prince had made the

30

beauty of that yard and flower beds the central interest of his life. He mowed and raked, edged and mulched, trimmed and planted, and tended that yard, keeping it at a level of perfection that few, if any, neighbors could, or would, afford. Flowers bloomed in their proper season in precise and orderly formations.

The distinctive appearance which marked the Oldham home was matched by the stately bearing and mannerisms of Major Oldham, the master of the house. The origin of the title "Major" was never made clear to me. Major Oldham seemed too old to have served in World War I, but could have served in the Spanish-American War. He seemed unlikely to have been a member of the National Guard. Major Oldham was an attorney and appeared to have sufficient economic means to sustain the stature and affectations of a "distinguished gentleman." Wearing a hat and carrying a gold-headed cane, he customarily walked the five blocks between his home and his office on the courthouse square. On such walks he scarcely spoke to or acknowledged the presence of those he met. Most of the people he met were not Republicans.

Major Oldham, in the 1920s, had a well-polished black sedan, one of the more expensive automobiles. It was usually parked in the driveway or garage of his home. I could not recall ever having seen him drive the car, yet no chauffeur drove it either. Mrs. Oldham or his daughter Dorothy did the driving. In this regard he fell a little short of another lawyer who had a chauffeur. Despite this minor diminution of dignity, Mr. Oldham seemed to have ample financial means with which to maintain a lifestyle befitting the upper level of the Oxford social structure.

I learned later that Mr. Oldham served as United States district attorney whenever a Republican was elected president of the United States. It was widely whispered that when a Republican president entered the White House, Mr. Oldham became even more important to those who aspired to be a postmaster or to be appointed to any other federal job in Mississippi; that, in fact, he was "the man to see."

Some who knew Mr. Oldham well described him as "pompous" and as "arrogant." From his appearance, bearing, and demeanor, I later would suspect that Mr. Oldham's ancestors had come from the British Isles, but from some point which was a little closer to the Crown, or other power center, than had the ancestors of most of the people of Oxford. What fortuitous circumstance brought this Republican into the post-Civil War political and social order of the South and Oxford, I never learned.

Although Major Oldham was a graduate of the Law School of the University of Mississippi, his affiliation with the Republican Party ("Black and Tan" or otherwise) was not the usual course for graduates of that school of law during this period. Mrs. Oldham, well-spoken, round of face, and with a ready smile showing teeth almost too perfect for nature's own creation, was not quite like the usual "southern lady." She exhibited a poise and bearing which may have been given to her by heritage, custom, habit, or training. She had attended the Cincinnati Conservatory of Music and sometimes taught piano lessons. She was friendly and personable.

My attention was suddenly drawn back to the refrigerator crate in the Oldham's yard for it appeared to be moving. As I came closer, it opened up. To my great dismay, out of it came a crowd of children. Some I knew; others were strangers. "Itsy" (Mary Elizabeth) Glenn and John Reed Holley were neighborhood kids. The other two were identified as "Cho Cho" and her little brother, Malcolm. Later I learned that Cho Cho's real name was Victoria De Graffenreid Franklin.

I quickly caught on to several things: Malcolm and Cho Cho had come from some far off place called Shanghai in China, which was on the other side of the world. They had left their father there, and their mother was Miss Estelle, the older daughter of Mr. and Mrs. Oldham. They were to stay in Oxford indefinitely. Last, but by no means least important, (for it was repeated several times among the children, and more or less confirmed by the nervous glances by the grown folks out of the front door and windows, with some occasional questions between adults and children as to what could be seen up toward town) that something important was about to happen. I learned, as the air of expectancy heightened, that "Mr. Billy" Falkner was coming!

Later I learned from my Aunt Ila and my older sister, Anna Mae, who were contemporaries of Mr. Billy, that he and Miss Estelle had been far more than mere acquaintances during their teenage years. Mr. Billy had lived in the third house north of the Oldham's home and east of his grandfather's home, but his frequent changing of jobs and traveling about had brought the Oldham family to the conclusion that he would never amount to much. Like many Oxford girls, Miss Estelle had become interested in "university boys," specifically, one Cornell Franklin from Columbus, Mississippi, who was a law student whose family owned property interests in Mississippi and in the Philippines. With much encouragement from the Oldham family he had won her heart and she had married Cornell and had gone to live in the Orient and had resided for a number of years in Shanghai, where Cornell had a substantial law practice, mainly representing business interests. After Miss Estelle's marriage, Mr. Billy had gone to New Haven, Connecticut, and later had joined the Royal Canadian Air Force during World War I. He had worked in New York, served as postmaster at the University of Mississippi, and had written a book.

Miss Estelle had returned to her Oxford home, without her husband, and now, after several years of being far apart, Mr. Billy and Miss Estelle were both back at their homes in Oxford. They were about to end their long separation.

As my friends and I played in and around the refrigerator box, I felt an unusual feeling of interest in and curiosity about Cho Cho. I felt a compulsion to watch her and her every move. Emotions surged within my small body. I was smitten with my first "crush" on a little girl from a far off, mysterious sounding place, which had stirred my imagination.

Cho Cho had dark-brown, straight hair which clung close to her head, giving her an almost oriental look, somewhat like the girls in movies about China which I had seen. Her brown and lively eyes were set in a thinnish face, with cheekbones a bit wider than her forehead and a slightly receding chin, all petite, pretty, and different. She moved with considerable grace and assurance in a willowy and gliding motion which gave the appearance of flowing here and there such as one might expect of a great ballerina. Her movements were distinctly different from the more abrupt and bouncy movements which I had observed in girls who had been reared in the local area. She had a lot of sophistication and mystique for a five year old.

Malcolm was a very small boy with a head that seemed a little too narrow at the top and bottom. From the hairline of his forehead down to his wider cheek bones, then down to his mouth and chin, Malcolm resembled his sister. Both Cho Cho and Malcolm possessed a quality of quiet reserve and dignity, a bit unusual for children of such tender years. Possibly they were reacting to their new surroundings with caution. While both differed from the local children in manner, appearance, and speech, this might have been attributable to their early years in a culture so different from that in which the rest of my friends had spent their earlier lives. Such differences had no great or lasting importance, however, and all but disappeared in the frolicking children's play. Within a few days they seemed as "natural" and "normal" as longtime friends could be.

"Here he comes!"

I could not be certain who said it, but I turned to see what was the subject of the exclamation. I beheld with considerable wonder what appeared to be a new and different type of man approaching upon the sidewalk of my hometown.

Mr. Billy wore a black derby hat, a black frock tailed coat, black bow tie, black trousers, and well-shined black shoes. A white flower protruded from the lapel of the coat. The black walking cane Mr. Billy carried was hooked over his left arm a little above the wrist and never touched the ground. The center of attention came on with deliberate but casual steps, not in haste or haltingly, just step by even step.

If Mr. Billy were even conscious of the gawking children playing around the refrigerator box giving him intensive scrutiny, he gave no sign. No doubt he knew that he was also being watched from behind the curtained windows of the Oldham's house, but he appeared completely oblivious of all who might be watching him, as if he neither knew nor cared and was preoccupied with some great undertaking. Indeed, time would prove the importance of his mission.

This man was not tall, only about five feet, five inches, more or less. The line of a dark moustache showed above his lip and it ascended to an apex beneath his nose.

He walked at an unhurried steady gait, not with the bobbing motion of the farmer crossing cotton rows, or with the urgency of the businessman getting to the bank before closing time. No quickened step, like the youthful lover approaching his girlfriend's door, revealed a nervous anticipation. He walked with purposeful steps, each as if a single note in a symphonic flow leading inexorably to a climactic chord. He looked into the distance appearing unaware, or uncaring, of all who might be watching.

Arriving at the two-step elevation to the Oldham's circling sidewalk, Mr. Billy casually turned to the left and ascended the steps.

With majestic dignity he moved along the circling walkway which led to the Oldham's front porch. He proceeded purposefully across the porch and knocked upon the Oldham's door. The door was opened, and, as Mr. Billy removed his hat and extended his hand in greeting, he passed through the door and out of my view.

Chapter 2
Party Time

The social life in a small Mississippi town like Oxford in the 1920s sometimes approached the bland. A considerable occasion might be a social at the Baptist Young People's Union (the B.Y.P.U.) with predictably delicious food and hot chocolate and, on rare occasions, a dish of ice cream. Excitement could be had for the price of a ticket to a picture show at the Lyric Theater, by far the most important nonreligious social center in those pretelevision days. A picture show coming to town called *The Road to Ruin* was a matter only to be whispered about. In this movie a girl became pregnant out of wedlock. Parents checked the daily comings and goings of children in an effort to prevent their slipping away to see such trash. Ministers railed upon the decline of morals and social order.

This even pre-dated radio dramas so not even the diversion of the great soap opera helped to while the time away. Few, indeed, even owned a radio. One could rarely escape the torturous tasks of learning reading, writing, and arithmetic, and the school year seemed unending.

While this scanty social life brought boredom to the older boys and girls, they, at least, had the comfort of reading novels and the Mid-South edition of the Memphis *Commercial Appeal.* In later years, the afternoon newspaper, the *Memphis Press-Scimitar,* gave them even more to think upon or talk about.

To those then five or eight, not yet old enough to be chasing girls, not smart enough to read very much, not rich enough to go to the movies, and not brave enough to venture out beyond the light of fading day, there was a problem called "what to do."

Much of this problem began to disappear when Cho Cho came to town with her mother, Miss Estelle, and little brother, Malcolm. They had seen and done many things that were unknown to local folks.

It was not unusual for a group to gather, as if by accident, around the Oldham's front steps on the way home after school, and any other time the opportunity occurred, to learn of what might be going on and to hope that something might be stirring.

Situated as it was on the east side of South Lamar, the Oldham house was directly on my route to and from town. There was really no way I could have conveniently avoided passing it even had I chosen to do so. Thus it was a happy time when an impromptu gathering of little boys and girls just appeared there, as if by some instinct, to chat and play and socialize at this "accidental" meeting place.

My initial crush on Cho Cho had quickly ripened into a love affair, at least so far as my dreams acted out the part. Never did I pass that house without the hope that Cho Cho might be outside.

As school progressed and playlets were staged, Cho Cho was often asked to get out her kimonos and play the part of a little Japanese or Chinese girl, the distinction being of no concern to me or to most of those who might have known that there was a difference between the two.

She and Itsy Glenn became fast friends and drifted off to such things as taking piano lessons and sharing little refinements that boys scarcely understood or cared about.

It was a great surprise when I was told by Cho Cho that soon there would be a garden party at the Oldham house, and I was invited to attend. Most of the children of nearby blocks were invited to be there at four o'clock. On learning this, my mother set about to get me properly attired for the party. A suitable fitting of knee-length trousers must be had together with a shirt to match. New shoes and socks were certainly a must, no matter what the cost.

So it was that on the appointed day, the small guests gathered at their accustomed place of play. It was a far more formal party than I had anticipated. I was fascinated by the grown-ups who were there.

Mrs. Oldham, with rounded face all full of smiles, Miss Dorothy, Miss Estelle, and even Major Oldham were all there, as were several neighbors and a dozen or more children. The children were greeted with considerable formality by all of the adults. The grown folks even shook my small hand, as is done in a receiving line, and introduced me to the next person in line.

Miss Estelle appeared to be somewhat like a pretty bird, a composite of Major Oldham, Mrs. Oldham, Cho Cho, and Malcolm, without the cheekbones narrowing to her forehead which Malcolm had, leading to the suspicion that he must have acquired them from his father.

She was a woman in her late twenties or early thirties. Her long dark brown hair was done up in a hairdo which kept it fairly close to her head. She was a bit smaller of frame and bone than Mrs. Oldham or her sister, Dorothy, and I thought she possessed more refinement of speech, gesture, and bearing than most of the women who had grown up in Oxford. Perhaps Miss Estelle's travels and associations with diverse peoples had given her a special quality of grace and poise. She could make even a small boy like me feel tall as a tree as she recognized and called me by name in her softly spoken voice. Probably she would have been as much at ease in the company of presidents, kings, diplomats, and businessmen of the international set. She could have passed for a movie star. There was a hint of Mrs. Oldham's roundish face, but Miss Estelle's was more shapely, as it tapered towards her mouth, a smaller mouth and not so full of teeth. Her face rounded down to a smallish chin which she carried at a level which was not depressed as with shy or timid souls, nor yet so high as to evince excessive self-esteem. Her understanding brown eyes and friendly voice and easy gracefulness could cause the lowliest to feel good and the haughtiest to become genteel. Small wonder that this lovely lady could attract the admiring attentions of most any male, including Mr. Billy.

Few secrets really exist in a town the size of Oxford, and none do if more than one person knows. In the nature of romance between boy and girl, inevitably there are two who know. The word was quickly passed around that Mr. Billy and Miss Estelle were seeing each other with some frequency. These two were ideal subjects for gossip to feed upon, particularly because their earlier courtship had come to no satisfying resolution.

Miss Dorothy was taller than Miss Estelle and maybe ten years younger, that is, in her late teens or early twenties. She was long of leg, arm, and body, and she bent forward a little at the waist, as if to shorten her height. While resembling Miss Estelle about the face enough to ascertain that they were sisters, the resemblance ended when matters of voice, movements, dress, and activities were considered. Miss Dorothy was very much an outdoor girl given to playing tennis and golf, and she walked with a bobbing and lengthy stride. She gave the impression of being a true tomboy. She had almost none of the smoothly flowing female walk, bearing, and speech of Miss Estelle, who could flow from place to place, or stand in place with effortless ease, usually saying the proper things. Miss Dorothy had a playful way and could be counted on to take the lead in organizing and directing the children's games with as much enthusiasm as those who played. Often she was clad in a shirt and skirt and appeared ready for any sport. On the other hand, Miss Estelle was scarcely ever seen without being dressed as if going to a party or ready for guests to arrive.

Major Oldham, ramrod straight and about six feet tall had hair and a moustache of whitening gray. He was wearing an iron-gray suit which fit him as if it were tailor-made. Over his left wrist he carried a cane which showed a little gold around the crook. It was more for show than for support. It was his custom to walk along the sidewalk going home from town with the cane thus held, and with a panama hat upon his head in the summertime, creating the impression that here was a man of wealth, knowledge, power, and influence, and such appraisal would not have been far wrong so long as there was a Republican in the White House.

On this particular occasion, however, Major Oldham was as friendly and courteous as a man could be. In a less stiffened and almost informal way, he bowed from the waist to greet and shake diminuitive hands. Although he, unlike Miss Estelle, Mrs. Oldham, and Miss Dorothy, did not know each child by name, for most were not children of Republicans, he did manage to make all feel welcome and at ease.

As the children began to arrive and mill about, Miss Dorothy became the one in charge of a number of children's activities. Some games were old and others new, and some involved the pairing off of little boys and girls. I found myself always trying to get into a position where I would be paired off with Cho Cho, feeling a bit dispossessed if by chance someone else won that place. Such occurrence happened only rarely, for even at this age, one's preference in the mating game is somehow communicated no matter the subtlety of conscious acts.

The considerable formality in greeting, along with party clothes, tended to dampen the children's inclination to go running, jumping, and playing the far more boisterous games to which they were accustomed. After all, this was a high level social affair. We drifted, or were herded, to the back yard. There the lawn was perfectly manicured, and I could see a long way off, even to the hills a mile away across Birney's Branch Bottom. Everyone walked through orderly plantings of flowers and even plucked strawberries from creeping vines. Then we ate cake and ice cream. After another game or two of what I considered downright sissy games like Drop the Handkerchief, which kids never play unless "organized" by overly attentive adults, there came a lull in the program.

Mr. Billy did not appear at the party, which was a bit of a disappointment to me. Since first I had seen Mr. Billy, I had learned much more about him and had hoped he would be at the party. I guessed that Mr. Billy was away on great affairs of business or writing or somewhere which scarcely really troubled me. Perhaps he was working to assemble the funds which he might someday use to keep Miss Estelle and her children in a style to which she and they would like to become accustomed. I could not have guessed that Mr. Billy might have been painting university buildings or serving as its postmaster.

However that may have been, when the name of William Falkner came up around my home, my older sister, Anna Mae, aroused my curiosity when she told of her generation referring to him as "Count No-'Count," and I wondered just what she meant. My curiosity over this remark increased when my Aunt Ila would make similar deprecating remarks. Even then, Mr. Billy was a conversation piece, in ever-widening circles and more consistently among his peers, who, while not completely understanding or admiring him, appeared to feel that he was worth talking about.

As with all good things, the party had to end. Someone gave the message that it was time to go, and we began to drift reluctantly to tell Mrs. Oldham and the Major and Miss Estelle and Miss Dorothy what a good time we had had. The children went their separate ways to give a full report, under intensive questioning by waiting mothers and families, of what had transpired at the Oldham's party.

Good parties do not end when they are over. Sometimes a party is so great that the aura lingers far beyond its time and place, sometimes for hours, days, weeks, or years. As I headed home, I reviewed the whole affair. Pleasant reflections came as I skipped and jumped in rhythmic strides, up banks of lawns and down across the sidewalk, as I hopped over a hedge and picked up a rock from the graveled street and threw it at a distant bird. I whistled a tune and wondered when I might see Cho Cho again.

There would be recurring thoughts of this day as I would, in the snowy predawn air of winter mornings when delivering the newspaper to the Oldham's door, recall that I had once visited here as an honored guest. I fantasized, Wouldn't it be great if just once Cho Cho would be at the door to take the paper from my own hands.

At other times I would recall that one Christmas morn when a new red wagon was left for me by Santa Claus that I could scarcely wait until I could take it up the street and ride down the Oldham's driveway until Cho Cho came out to play. There would be times when, wearing sweaty and dirty overalls and pushing my lawnmower home after cutting some neighbor's grass, I would not want to be seen by Cho Cho or Miss Estelle in my worker's garb and would go a block or so out of my way to avoid the possibility of being seen. I would prefer to walk on the Oldham's side of the street when dressed for Sunday school or when I could ride a bike along the sidewalk and wave a hand for all to see.

On the night following the party, it was quite enough to contemplate what had really happened. Did Cho Cho really mean it when she had squeezed my hand or had stood by my side in line awaiting the ice cream? Was it possible that she might leave town as suddenly as she had come? Would Mr. Billy marry Miss Estelle so Cho Cho could stay nearby?

On this, like many other nights, I relived this day's delights as sleep merged reveries with dreams.

Chapter 3

Of Manuscripts and Turkish Blends

Time came rushing on and slipped away into history year by year. Mr. Billy had married Miss Estelle in 1929. His fame as a writer had increased. I heard that he had bought the old house in Bailey's Woods and was moving Miss Estelle, Cho Cho, and Malcolm there. I was now eleven years old, and I was growing up.

It came as a pleasant surprise when Cho Cho invited me to a party to be given in the new home which Mr. Billy had bought not long before. Party time was four o'clock. The party plans were that Miss Dorothy would pick me up at the corner of Johnson Avenue and South Lamar. It was only a block from my home.

My mother insisted that I wear my very best dress-up clothes, including long navy blue pants, a new white shirt, and even a tie; that I even had to brush my teeth, clean my fingernails, and wash my hands a second time after shining my new black shoes. It did seem to me that this was overdoing it somewhat, but in the gathering anticipation—and really having no choice—I did as my mother said.

I was at the appointed corner a few minutes before the scheduled time and looked north toward the square to see if I could see the Oldham's car approaching. Soon I identified the big, black, and shiny Chrysler coming down the street. It appeared to have a lot of heads bobbing about inside as children squirmed, looked from side to side in the car, and changed position every second or so to get a better view. Probably it was the first ride most had ever had in an automobile, and certainly it was the first time any had ever had the opportunity of riding in the Oldham's polished and plushy four-door Chrysler sedan.

I found a space, and Miss Dorothy drove on down south along Lamar until the car reached the bottom of the hill, and she turned west on the dirt surface of Garfield Avenue.

When the streets of Oxford had been renamed, the east-west streets were named avenues for the succession of U.S. presidents. Thus the one which was to the south of Lincoln, Johnson, Grant, and Hayes became Garfield Avenue. Later it would be renamed the Old Taylor Road. To long-time residents of Oxford, it made little difference what the streets and avenues were named, or renamed, for these older settlers called the streets by their original names. In Johncy Falkner's book, *my Brother Bill,* he still refers to Lake Street and Second South Street. That book was published in 1964, more than thirty years after the names were changed.

Miss Dorothy, of course, knew where she was going, and as she turned right on Garfield Avenue, I could only see the honeysuckle-covered hillside of the Pegues's lot, then the one-room frame servant's house which stood a few feet from the south side of the road. She drove up a little incline, and the car was on a level with an expanse of open ground to the south. I recognized this as a part of the Elliott home, said to have been the home of Jacob Thompson before the Civil War, and more recently sometimes called the Elliott-Howorth home. The grounds of that home included about twenty acres.

The Elliott's land was familiar to me as a favorite playing field, where on many afternoons I had played baseball. Between that open ground and the Pegues's home, back to the east, was another familiar haunt, for there grew the most profuse honeysuckle vines I had ever encountered. They had grown there for many years, and they were so thick and springy that the smaller, or even middle-sized, boys could jump off the top of the bank supporting the up-

46

permost vines and bounce and roll and tumble downward for at least twenty-five feet until the bottom of the gully was reached without a broken arm or neck.

As we moved west we passed the front of the Elliott's home with its driveway bordered by cedar trees that sloped upward to the house situated at the highest point on the ridge.

Then I could see the corner of Garfield Avenue where it joined the "old road to Taylor," as it was then called. While I had only a general idea of where I was going, I knew that Mr. Billy's new house was in Bailey's Woods, and perhaps I had even passed in front of it without seeing much of it, for the house was three or four hundred feet from the street in the dark shadows of cedar trees. Probably none of those in the car had yet seen the house itself at close range, as we were about to do. At this corner there was an opening in the thickly grown forest which became a trail and was the entrance into Bailey's Woods. The trail ran straight ahead to the west and, if followed for a few hundred yards, would take the traveler deep into the hundred or more acres of the University Woods. In the northwest quadrant of the corner was the entrance to Mr. Billy's grounds.

Here it was that Mr. Billy was destined to live for more than thirty years, thereby giving it a lasting place in the annals of literature.

When my friends and I in the Oldham car arrived at Mr. Billy's home, we felt the anticipation that always seems to be generated when a party has just begun. I felt more at ease when I saw Itsy Glenn, Arthur Guyton, John Reed Holley, and Malcolm Franklin.

The little girls were dressed in party gowns of frilly, lacy, netty, and fluffy stuff which, while not full length, came well below their knees.

We looked and strolled around the spacious lawn and woods beyond before the fun got "organized." Such games as Post Office and Clap In and Clap Out required boys and girls to hint of favorites and, as youthful couples, to disappear together, perhaps for a walk all the way around the house. Some even held hands and took their time. Others were full of nervous chatter and almost ran the course. Whether to show the chaperones that they had not been gone long enough to "make love," or to take a chance upon getting a more attractive partner, never was made quite clear.

Tempted to explore, several of the boys, including me, went into the house and into the west room on the downstairs floor, just inside the front hall door, and looked about to see what might be seen. I noticed a very old typewriter on a table. This, according to Malcolm, was the typewriter that Mr. Billy used in typing most of his writings.

Malcolm, now seven or eight years old, picked up a shaggy pack of papers, which seemed to be the makings of a book, and said that this was something Mr. Billy was writing. It was called a "manuscript," and when he got through with it and sent it away to a publisher, the publisher would not be able to change a single word, not even so much as a comma. Mr. Billy would not let the publisher print it if he changed his writing in any way.

Before we left Mr. Billy's writing room, Malcolm, with mischievously sparkling eyes, turned and said, "Look here at these new cigarettes of Mr. Billy's." Like the rest, I looked and pondered and smelled and felt and put them down and picked them up again. The print on the package said they were made of "Turkish blends." Then several of the boys, in unspoken conversation, framed a common question with glances at each other: I wonder what it would be like to smoke a Turkish cigarette?

It wasn't that the tobacco smelled good or, for that matter, particularly bad. It wasn't that any of us had a desire to smoke, because the most that we knew of smoking at that tender age was that the preacher said it was a bad thing, and we would not dare to let our mothers know that the thought of smoking anything had ever crossed our minds. Still, I, like some of the others, had puffed on a grape vine joint, corn silks, or rabbit tobacco rolled inside a piece of paper a time or two. Curiosity and the spirit of adventure commanded an experiment.

Someone came up with a match, and we lit one of those cigarettes. We passed the thing around, and puffed and coughed a little. I noticed that the world started to go around. Then with great panic I wondered how we would hide the evidence of our misdoings, the cigarette butt, lest we be found out by anyone who cared.

Rowan Oak, 1930
William Faulkner's home before renovation. Built about 1844 for the Shegog family, it is situated on fourteen acres of land and is now owned by the University of Mississippi.

Time had quickly passed while we boys were having our adventure. Now it was time to go back out to the yard before someone might ask where we had been, or worse, what we had been doing.

Someone called, and we went outside and along a brick walkway which led out from the front door steps to the narrow carriage driveway. Just to the left of the walk everyone sat on the ground in a circle beneath the cedar trees. I stole a sideways glance to see if anyone might be staring at my guilty face. I still was feeling the effects of my experience with the Turkish blended cigarette and I felt a little queasy. I hoped I was not getting sick.

There were some magazines piled near the driveway, and some were as thick as books and had paper backs, resembling those I had peeped into at the drug store. They sometimes told of wild Western tales, of cowboys and horses and mountain trails, but these particular ones told tales of adventure and heroics during World War I. One, in particular, was making the rounds. It was entitled *Canadian Aces.*

Now all who knew Mr. Billy, or had heard of him, knew that he had spent some time in the Canadian military service and in the flying part of it, and I thought that maybe Mr. Billy had been reading of the exploits of his comrades in arms.

Someone said, "Oh look, here is a story by Mr. Billy," and look everyone did and tried to get a better view and to read a little before the next one grabbed it. The excitement grew as all realized that we were there in the yard of a person who had written stories for so glamorous a publication as *Canadian Aces*. The seed was firmly planted in every mind that they wanted to know more.

Cho Cho asked, "Would you like to have Mr. Billy tell us a story?" The automatic yes was heard, and she went off and found Mr. Billy. Everyone got as quiet as they had ever been, and Mr. Billy began to tell us a tale.

The story took place at about the time of the Civil War when a girl, who had lived at this very house, had fallen in love with a Yankee soldier. She was killed when she fell from her bedroom window while going out to meet him, and at times the sounds of her ghost playing the piano might still be heard. The story was full of suspense and mystery, and Mr. Billy gave a great performance. His eyes seemed to pierce every child as he gestured with his hands, his voice rising with excitement, then falling to a whisper as he neared the story's end. When he was finished, all seemed entranced. Then someone asked that he do another one, and he obliged, and it was just as good. Everyone clapped, and he looked pleased and bowed, then disappeared as suddenly as he had appeared.

It was time for cookies, cake, and ice cream which all ate, and ate again. Finally I felt I was almost over-filled.

By then the shadows had deepened, as they do in a cedar-shaded yard, and the sun had sunk low in the west through the University Woods. Probably no one relished the thought of walking in the darkening woods or along the streets of Oxford to their homes. It occurred to me that darkness might overtake me on the way. I was not sure about how I would get home, for nothing had been said about that.

As if part of a master plan, however, Miss Dorothy gathered a car full of kids, including me, and said she would take us home, or nearly so. She let me out of her car close to my home well before dark, when my mother might begin to worry.

Burdened with apprehension, I carefully kept away from everyone at home, staying as far away from my mother as possible. I hoped to limit the chances of her all-knowing motherly instincts detecting, by my guilty or excessively innocent look, or tobacco scent, that I had been smoking a cigarette.

In the next few years other parties would be given at Mr. Billy's home, later to become known as Rowan Oak. It was a happy time, this middle phase of growing up. The more daring and adventuresome boys sometimes whispered that under the big magnolia tree could be found a little drink of gin, though that was never the proper thing to do for those who feared detection and disaffection or being "talked about." Some of my friends and I were Boy Scouts.

Cigarette smoking, on the other hand, had become an accepted thing, when out of the presence of the grown-up folks. Often we boys would go out in the yard in turns to take a puff on a cigarette as the chance appeared.

By these early teenage years, the mating instinct became more evident. It caused a greater scatteration of the young guests who strolled about the grounds to where a large tree might conceal a stolen kiss as the pairing off began. By now the parties were mostly at night, and murmuring sounds could be heard in the darker, more secluded places. Occasionally couples would return to the house with tousled hair or smeared lipstick, and grassy stains on knees or seats.

Cho Cho's parties were not confined to the grounds of Rowan Oak, for in the middle teenage years, once when the Oldhams were out of town, she, like teenagers everywhere, invited a few friends in to enjoy her grandparents' home. This was the first time I had ever really roamed through that immaculate mansion. There were some who "smooched" in darker alcoves and even on the stairs.

By 1933, the crowd was growing up. New faces began to appear, as might be expected in a university town, as families came and went. I was reaching the age when girls mature faster than do their male contemporaries and find more interest in older boys, dropping their childhood friends in favor of more sophisticated college men, particularly those from distant places, no matter whether from towns great or small, like Duck Hill, Alligator, Jackson, or even Vicksburg. From the last named town would come a college man whose arrival in Oxford would forever change the history of Mr. Billy's family, and Cho Cho's life. His name was Claude Selby.

Thus it was, that the glorious period of life began to fade away. The little girls began to find that young love's fun and play had been only training them for the mating game.

Cho Cho went off to Mississippi Synodical College at Holly Springs, a Presbyterian version of the "finishing school," after she graduated from high school. This thirty-mile separation from the Ole Miss campus was not far enough from the Ole Miss boys, for Claude Selby found and married her before she finished her first year of college. That event brought an end to my attendance at the parties at Mr. Billy's house.

As of the time of my encounter with my first cigarette and my holding of one of Mr. Billy's manuscripts, it would have seemed preposterous to have imagined that I might again see that manuscript and that old Underwood typewriter in the same position on the same table fifty years later.

Chapter 4

The Poacher's Retreat

It was an October afternoon in 1933 when a tinge of yellow had begun to appear in the leaves of the hickory trees. School had started but had lost its novelty after the first few weeks, and my fantasies turned to roaming in the woods. I thought of feigning illness to escape football practice just for one day, and I became preoccupied with avoiding the coach, my teachers, and anyone else who might distract my mind from its craving for the outdoors, roaming in the forest, and hearing woodland noises. I almost became a victim of such a distraction when the beautiful and shapely blonde who sat facing me in the class crossed her legs, and I saw the flash of her pink slip as she settled into her new position, but I quickly diverted my gaze to the clock which ever more slowly moved toward the end of the class. Finally the school bell rang, and I was free at last.

It was such a beautiful day that I jogged the mile or so to my home. En route I planned my rare escape from a world which increasingly had hemmed me in. I entered the house dropping books and papers, took off my school clothes, and pulled on an old sweater and ragged hunting pants.

Two things could not be resisted, however, regardless of the press of time. First was a piece of my mother's cold cornbread, sweetened by an onion and softened by a glass of buttermilk, which I munched upon the back steps as the sun began to angle toward the west. The second indispensable was a very old .22-caliber rifle and a dozen or so cartridges. The rifle was a single shot Stevens, the breech of which opened by a lever which covered the trigger. It must have been a popular model and design some time around the early 1900s.

The rifle was one my older brother had used when he was a boy, and it had a defect: the firing pin was worn and would not dependably fire the cartridge. Often after patiently stalking game and aiming carefully, the pull of the trigger only produced a click, but I had to accept this frustrating experience if I were to hunt at all.

In 1933, the boys of Oxford more or less presumed, if they ever even thought about it at all, that they had hunting rights on any land where the owners allowed trees, bushes, vines, or sedge grass to grow up into a bramble where birds and squirrels and rabbits might make their homes. I could not recall ever having asked a property owner if I might hunt upon his land—not because I feared rejection of my request, but because the thought just never entered my mind that anyone would object, or that the owner had a right to do so.

When the hunting season opened, it would be the usual thing for several teenage hunters to be observed in a single afternoon around the favorite hunting spots. Rarely, if ever, was there concern for the possibility that a rifle bullet might travel far beyond the intended target, might ricochet in unintended directions, might kill a neighbor's cow, or strike some person along the way. This did not usually happen, or if it did, the very number of youngsters in the woods would have made it difficult to determine the suspects, much less the guilty party.

As I finished my cornbread, onion, and buttermilk, the sun was leaning toward the west, and I realized that I must be off to see what I could find, to breathe the cooling air of fall, and to seek adventure before the day was gone.

I strode down through the pasture, but no wild game stirred. I came to the back fence which was along a closed right of way for Garfield Avenue, now blocked on the east side of South Lamar by the house of Mr. Bryan Tate, a house which I had helped build. As

Mr. Jenks Cullen was pouring the concrete for the first full basement I had ever seen being constructed, he had let me, as a ten-year-old, shovel some sand and gravel into the concrete mixer. Now this house blocked my path on a westerly course, but not for long. The house was built on a lot which had been graded flat. A steep bank descended to a ravine and on that bank grew a bramble of Himalaya vines, which, in addition to controlling erosion, offered protection for rabbits and birds and wild life in general.

Where South Lamar crosses the little ravine, about a hundred feet to the north of the briar patch, there was a square concrete culvert, about three feet wide and deep, designed to drain an area of about sixty or more acres of land which sloped at diverse angles toward the ravine. To the west someone had a garden planted on the rich alluvial soil which had settled there as rain waters waited to gain access to the culvert.

To avoid climbing the steeply sloping bank up to South Lamar, I decided to retrace the steps of former years when I was considerably smaller and when I had often crawled through the culvert. Upon a sudden impulse, I entered the culvert which traversed about fifty feet to the other side of the street above and to the garden plot.

Suddenly, I realized that I was no longer a boy of ten. Nature had done strange things to my size by the time I had reached fourteen, adding a foot or so until I had attained my present six feet in height. Nevertheless, the course was set and in something between walking and crawling on my hands and knees, I managed to get into the culvert. I felt a slight feeling of panic about halfway through as I recalled tales of cave explorers being caught in such a passage where they could go neither forward nor backward. The panic passed, however, and I reached the other side. I walked on the tops of garden rows until I reached the edge of Garfield Avenue, later to be known as the Old Taylor Road, and continued west for about a quarter of a mile.

Bailey's Woods stood at the southwest corner of the Old Taylor Road and Garfield Avenue, and extended to the west of the road. On entering Bailey's Woods, there was a thicket of great density, of smallish trees and scrub brush and blackberry vines with an occasional cedar tree and oaks and perhaps of greatest importance, a "hickernut tree."

Most would call the latter a hickory tree, but colloquial English, being as it was, everyone knew the meaning and was satisfied with the description of a "hickernut tree." Such trees dotted the hills and hollows of sandy clay of the entire region and were a favorite source of wood for a bow and arrow which small boys made when playing games of fantasy about the Indians who had once lived there.

While several hickernut trees were to be found about Bailey's Woods, there was one in particular which seemed to be the father of the forest and so dominated that woodland that other large trees kept their distance. About four feet across the trunk at the base, it

Bailey's Woods
Generations of youthful hunters have roamed these woods, sometimes poaching William Faulkner's squirrels. The property lies south of Rowan Oak and is bordered by Old Taylor Road and University Woods. In 1937, William Faulkner published an appeal for the hunters to stop shooting his tame squirrels.

Photo courtesy of Herman E. Taylor

rose to stretch its branches outward fifty feet or more. Little grew beneath the great tree save sassafras, honeysuckle, a cedar or two, and the little dogwoods which seemed to savor the shelter of the larger tree. In between these smaller growths was a pithy mat of fallen rotted leaves and crackly limbs and the hulls of nuts from years gone by all mixed in a mulchy pad.

My goal was a strategic point up close to the hickory tree, not too close nor yet too far. Squirrels are a suspicious lot and prone to disappear at the slightest unusual human noise they hear. I avoided an easier approach which would have been down the trail in front of Mr. Billy's house and instead took a circuitous course, a hundred feet to the south of the trail. From this direction the light from the slanting sun would aid me in spotting any movement in the hickory tree which might tell me of any squirrel up there in the tree.

I stealthily stepped and stopped and stepped and listened and stepped again upon the carpeted forest floor until I could see the full spread of the hickory tree. Then I sat down and lay flat upon the ground with my rifle loaded and cocked and ready for action.

Squirrels are improvident critters. They could wait for nutsto mature and have ample food for eating all winter long; instead, they strip off nuts which are barely in the milky stage with little solid matter to eat and drop the hulls and remains on the ground. Whether the nuts are pecans, scaley barks, or hickernuts their habits seem the same. I figured that on such a day some squirrel would most likely be about the tree.

A few minutes after I had taken my position, my heart leaped with excitement for I did indeed see a movement in the hickory tree. Without moving a muscle, I saw a squirrel glide up the trunk and around it to a large limb running northward from the trunk toward the land in front of Mr. Billy's house. The squirrel climbed to successively smaller limbs until he reached the nuts hanging there. He helped himself so far as I could see, but my view was somewhat obscured by the leaves. I thought I would wait a moment for a clearer view and for the squirrel to stop moving since a .22-rifle is not the best weapon with which to try to hit a moving target.

In a moment the squirrel came into sight as it returned to the larger limb and stopped to eat his nut. By then I had leveled my gun upon the spot, and as the squirrel crawled along on the limb, he came within my gun sight and I squeezed the trigger.

I rose halfway from the ground, froze in fright, then sagged back to the ground for I sensed a movement to my right. I had thought that I was alone in the woods for my game of stalking and shooting squirrels, but this proved not to be the case.

The movement which had caused my fright came from across the trail. In shocked surprise of panic proportions I beheld standing there none other than Mr. Billy Faulkner.

Mr. Billy had a pipe in his mouth and a hand on one hip. He had instantly materialized, it seemed, from nowhere when he had heard my rifle shot. He stood at his fence line, and his eyes narrowed into slits as he searched the woods from right to left. He studied the underbrush up and down, then he moved a few feet to the side as he continued to examine the mass of foliage in the thicket.

I lowered my head close to the ground and scarcely breathed at all for what seemed an endless time.

Mr. Billy continued his intense scrutiny and shifted his position and looked some more. I hoped that I had blended with the undergrowth into invisibility. As time wore on, sweat poured down my face and trickled down my neck. Finally Mr. Billy turned and began to walk slowly toward his house.

The emotional surf that swept over me, feelings of guilt and fear of possible detection by Mr. Billy, caused me to lie there motionless for awhile. I had always greatly admired Mr. Billy, and the thought of being caught by him drained me of the hunter's urge. I felt that I was now the hunted. I felt like a murderer must who, after having fired the fatal bullet, discovers that he has been observed while doing his deadly deed.

It had never even occurred to me to wonder whose land I was hunting on, or whether I was on Mr. Billy's property. Nevertheless, I felt that Mr. Billy would not have been so intent in looking for me unless he had some interest in that land. I knew, of course, that I did not want to be caught by Mr. Billy and have to face him after having done this poacher's deed.

While not inclined to leave the squirrel, if indeed I had killed it, the countervailing impulse was to get out of there, and it became an irresistible urge.

At this point a rush of foreboding crowded into my mind. If I should venture out on the trail and on down Garfield Avenue, possibly Mr. Billy would drive along and, putting two and one together, meaning rifle and rifle shot and boy walking near the woods, I would be undone. Mr. Billy would have no doubt as to the poacher's identity.

That could not be. Then what? Even if Mr. Billy did not personally see me walking there with my gun, would someone else see and tell? All-seeing eyes and wagging tongues leave few secrets in small towns.

These thoughts so cluttered and confused my mind that I came close to paranoia.

The deepening shadows let me know that it was more than time to go home. Such time constraint limited my choice of routes.

I could have waited until dark and skulked along the darker streets avoiding street lights to reach the safety of my mother's house. By then, however, she, with great concern for my safety on such a hunt, might cause the alarm to spread too far. I could go deeper into the woods in a southerly direction, so as to keep Mr. Billy from seeing me emerge from the woods, for I imagined that Mr. Billy would keep a sharp lookout to see whom he might see, and with a good possibility that he would be seeing me. Thus, the choice forced me to go much deeper into the woods and cross the Old Taylor Road down below the hill to the south of the Elliott home beyond the city limits and down near the valley bottom.

Going east I crossed over, under, or through numerous barbed wire fences and finally reached South Lamar, a half mile to the east, and south of Guy McLarty's home. Then I reached the little stream which made a valley to the east of South Lamar. It flowed from the north and passed through Tate's pasture and more familiar ground. Eventually I reached the haven of my mother's pasture and felt that I had found a refuge from a perverse and hostile world.

As night began to fall, I came to the steps of my back porch and heard some of life's most welcome sounds, those of my mother and sister talking about what they had fixed for supper.

While waiting for supper to be readied, I went down and sat on the bottom step and contemplated and wondered how it could be said that shooting defenseless little animals, which could not shoot back, was "sport." I recalled a verse I had learned in Sunday school which says, "God sees the little sparrow fall."

I wondered whether I had killed the squirrel or missed him entirely.

I looked up toward the early stars in the darkening sky to the east as I meditated upon the meanings of adventure, sport, life, and death. I tried to decide whether I was more depressed because I may have killed the squirrel or because I had almost been caught in doing so by Mr. Billy.

Mr. Billy's troubles with poachers did not end with my withdrawal from that activity. Others took my place. A few years later, Mr. Billy published a short message in *The Oxford Eagle*, the town's newspaper, in which he entreated one and all to leave his squirrels alone and to stop shooting near his cow's pasture and his home. The message read as follows:

Notice

The posted woods on my private property inside the City limits of Oxford contain several tame squirrels. Any hunter, who feels himself too lacking in woodcraft and marksmanship to approach a dangerous wild squirrel, might feel safe with them.

These woods are a part of a pasture used by my horses and milk cow; also, the late arrival will find them already full of other hunters. He is kindly requested not to shoot either of these.

—William Faulkner

In later years, as live and shooting Japanese lurked just outside the perimeter of far Pacific battlefields, I would recall and try to duplicate the breathless stillness and tricks of camouflage which I had practiced in avoiding detection by Mr. Billy beneath the great hickory tree. I did not consider whether I was engaged in a "sport," but I knew well that I was having an "adventure."

Chapter 5

Bourbon and Alabaster

The train had bumped and rocked, slowed and accelerated, stopped and backed, started and switched, and changed directions throughout the night as it transported my company from the Desert Training Center near Yuma, Arizona, to its new station. I had been assigned to duty as officer of the day and had been awake much of the night as events arose which required my attention. As dawn began to arrive, I looked out. I could scarcely believe what I saw. My first impression was that, while there might be a prettier place on Earth, I had never seen it.

In late February the mountains near San Luis Obispo, California, were covered almost to their tops with a deep green carpet of grass. Small trees grew near the summits of some of these mountains as was true of the mountain just to the south of Camp San Luis Obispo.

My impression of the beauty of that scenery was heightened on that morning in 1943 because I had recently completed about six months of army maneuvers. The first few months had been in the cedar-covered countryside near Lebanon, Tennessee, where limestone bedrock was sometimes only a few inches beneath the topsoil.

More recently, there had been maneuvers over the sand and gravel surfaces of the desert to the west of Yuma, Arizona. The campsite had been a mile or so from the All-American Canal which flowed out of the Colorado River at a dam north of Yuma.

The maneuvers went over the land from near the Mexican border for about a hundred miles to the north and northwest. Armored divisions and motorized infantry divisions, including tens of thousands of men and thousands of trucks, tanks, jeeps, and half-tracks prepared for combat in the African desert. They churned the desert crust which had been formed over many years into clouds of suffocating dust. The gravel surface crust had been left as the dust had been blown away, and strong winds created dust storms out of the underlying soil.

The Sixth Motorized Infantry Division of the U.S. Army was being trained and prepared to fight a desert war. Its future was changed with the defeat of the German General Rommel's Afrika Korps by Montgomery's British troops at El Alamein. Thus the Sixth Division was changed into a jungle fighting infantry division destined for combat in the New Guinea and the Philippine campaigns.

The overnight ride on the troop train had been surprisingly comfortable. There was a bed for each GI on board. This seemed almost too good to be true following what had seemed an endless succession of nights on maneuvers of sleeping on the ground and wiggling to find the most comfortable position among the rocks on the desert. I remembered shivering in the November cold in Tennessee after General Ben Lear ordered all winter clothing and sleeping bags returned to the division's base at Fort Leonard Wood, Missouri. I speculated that the general must have thought that requiring soldiers to wear summer-weight uniforms in the winter weather would toughen them up for the war.

I recalled that in the desert I had eaten canned food, dried and dehydrated potatoes, and "C" rations cooked over a number 10 can filled with sand and doused with gasoline.

I had looked around that morning and wondered for an instant whether I had died and gone to heaven as I had looked in awe at the beauty and vastness of the expanse of green grassland which seemed to ascend to the mountain tops and join the sky.

The good life of a garrison soldier was discovered a short time later when my company detrained and marched directly to a mess hall where, it seemed to me, some of the better army cooks had prepared one of the best breakfasts I had ever eaten. Food which I had almost forgotten about turned up before me. Fresh fruits and juices and bacon and eggs and GI bread and Golden State milk, all one could drink, were there for the taking.

San Luis Obispo is situated about halfway between San Francisco and Los Angeles. I remembered passing through San Luis Obispo in 1940 because it is the place where the Southern Pacific Railroad has in it what is called Horseshoe Bend as the railroad descends the mountains from the north of the city. I had been a newly commissioned second lieutenant, a recent graduate of the Ole Miss R.O.T.C. On that trip I had just returned from what was something of a luxury cruise aboard the U.S. Army transport *Leonard Wood* from Charleston, South Carolina, through the Panama Canal, to Hawaii, then to San Francisco.

On board was a considerable number of high-ranking army and navy officers.

Many of these officers would be stationed in Hawaii when the Japanese attacked Pearl Harbor. Some of the admirals and generals would find that their military careers had ended in disgrace in the smoke and flame of the initial battle of World War II.

That first trip through San Luis Obispo was something of a bonus and lark since I found that the Old Army of that pre-World War II era allowed about ten days for each officer to get to Cheyenne. This time was about evenly divided for sightseeing and recreation between San Francisco and the Los Angeles and Hollywood tourist attractions before taking the Union Pacific for a two-day chair car ride to Fort Warren. Chair car seats were as good as second lieutenants could afford after their unexpected visits to so many tourist traps. Also, the opportunities for social adventures were greater in coach seats than in a Pullman berth.

That had been in 1940, but this was 1943. The nation was at war, and an increased seriousness of purpose and maturity of mind had transformed those once footloose and fun-loving second lieutenants into more responsible officers who were now moving up the ranks to captain and major, and commanding troops who might soon be facing a shooting enemy in only God knew where.

About a month after the move to Camp San Luis Obispo, there came a call from division headquarters in which I was advised that

I had been promoted to captain. If there were ever a telephone call to gladden the heart of a soldier, being told of my promotion would be most likely to head the list.

I soon found that being the "commanding officer" required a lot of work and worry. I had something of an added burden by being a separate unit commander. While having considerable freedom to act on my own, I was ultimately responsible for nearly everything. I had to get the troops trained for every contingency. I was particularly plagued by the inspections of numerous staff officers who came too frequently to inspect. It seemed that whatever happened, or failed to happen, if good, was merely as expected, but if bad, was considered my fault.

As soon as I had received the call, I got my driver, Corporal Zimmerman, to drive me to the post exchange so I could get some captain's bars, the "parallel railroad tracks."

At that time Signal Corps officers wore woolen shirts with Signal Corps flags on the left side of the collar. The captain's insignia was on the right side. Then the field jacket required some railroad tracks on each shoulder. The overseas cap was the prescribed headgear; the fourth set of tracks was mounted there. As I looked into the mirror I thought I had never seen so much silver on one officer, but I confessed to myself that I was proud of all of that evidence of my new rank.

In a separate company such as the Sixth Signal Company it was not easy to gain promotion to the grade of captain, for there was only one captain with a dozen lieutenants wanting the job. I had finally outlasted all of those who had preceded me in rank. Now it was my duty and high calling to get my outfit ready for combat, that is, if I should last long enough as company commander.

I quickly began to feel, as I was bombarded by requirements and criticism and requests seemingly from every spoke of the wheel, that the entire United States was depending upon me to get this part of the army prepared to win the war. After all, in the chain of command there was the president, the army commander, the division commander, and Captain Taylor. When things went wrong, as they often did, I found that I was the one at the end of the chain who would receive the blame.

As chilly winds from the Monterey peninsula wafted over the coastal range and along the valleys, the penetrating fog seemed to come into the little "hutment" where I was quartered. These were tarpaper-covered wooden house frames about the size of a pyramidal tent. Each housed about six enlisted men or three officers. They were heated by kerosene heaters. Many, if not most, of the officers were married and had brought their wives to the nearby towns where living quarters could be found. They wanted to "go home" at night to their garage apartments, basement rooms, attic spaces, or beach houses situated within about twenty miles from camp. I, as one of the few unmarried officers, found it difficult to refuse to take their place as duty officer as I was asked to do on many nights. This did little to dispel my own loneliness during the nights and at the age of twenty-four, I sensed my need for something better. A weekend or two in Los Angeles kept me conscious of a great big wonderful world out there with places like the Palladium and Brown Derby, good hotels and pretty girls, and adventures to be had. It occurred to me that there must be something better than merely being a perpetual duty officer by night and a commanding officer by day and night.

Thus, when I got those captain's bars and was told that my pay would go up to about $370 per month, one of the first things to flash through my mind was, That may be enough to keep a woman.

In response to this inspiring revelation, and as if by unconscious reflex action, I got myself a pocket full of quarters and headed for the nearest pay telephone. A three-by-three-foot glass and wood pay telephone booth located beside a busy street between my company area and post headquarters is not at all like the kind of setting in which one would like to be when popping the most important question of his life. And telephone service during the war was uncertain. Could a long distance call get through? If so, would she be able to hear me? What should I say when propounding such a question to a girl as, Will you marry me?

Soon the operator got Nina Claire on the line. She had graduated a semester before her class by virtue of some summer school credits and had taken a job as a home economics teacher in Okolona, Mississippi, immediately after graduation in January. She had discovered that little girls in the seventh grade created problems for her. They had grown up in smaller towns and on farms and already were experienced in cooking and sewing. She had to resort to the method of Socrates and goad them with questions in order to cover up her lack of previous experience in the kitchen and at the sewing machine.

In Clarksdale, her home town in the Mississippi Delta, her mother had always had a cook named Bertha who had ruled the family kitchen from her earliest recollection. To Nina Claire, the thought of sewing and knitting and other feats of domesticity had never crowded out her natural tendency to be a "people's person." She could almost always get someone who could do it better to do what needed to be done. Thus it was that she came to Mississippi State College for Women and decided to major in Home Economics to learn what she had missed and, incidentally, to become employable.

By March, having been a teacher for more than a month, Nina Claire was thoroughly disenchanted, in particular with trying to show experts how to cut patterns or how to bake fluffy biscuits or a beautiful and tasty cheese soufflé. This preconditioning for a proposal of marriage I did not know about, although her letters had seemed to reflect a lack of enthusiasm for her job.

We had, of course, discussed the possibility of marriage upon our infrequent visits when I could get leave or when army orders permitted a detour to some meeting place often enough to keep aflame the mystical natural attraction which had instantly developed when we had first met in Clarksdale in 1939.

I was then in my senior year at the University of Mississippi. My dance band had played for the Odd Club dance in Clarksdale. A friend of Nina's, Martha Sessions, who lived across the street from Nina, was infatuated with a member of the band and staged a pre-dance supper for the members of the band. Nina Claire and I were late by exactly the same amount of time. We climbed the stairs, I following Nina, to hang up our coats. When she turned around in my direction, our eyes met for a moment and in that instant many messages passed between us. We instinctively turned and sauntered down the stairs together and thus became paired off for dinner.

She stood five feet four in height, brown of hair, neither dark or light, and skin tanned as if from having participated in outdoor sporting events. Her face was a little wider at the cheekbone level and narrower near the forehead, somewhat matching the narrowing down to her chin. She gave easy smiles to everyone she saw, and with darting eyes, she cased the entire crowd attending the party. She was the kind of girl, I thought, who would as appropriately fit into a garden dress, a kitchen apron, or in a formal gown at an inauguration. She would be a sparkplug in any conversation. She seemed as natural and earthy as the blooming rose. Her sparkling eyes kept moving here and there to see who and what was where. It seemed obvious to me that wherever she was, there also the action would be. She was the kind of girl who likely would be able to sew and cook a stew and do what else she needed to do and keep the fun alive as she attended to a brood of four or five children. She seemed to know most everyone there and strolled about with a pat for the girls and a kiss for the boys as though each was her favorite toy.

She and I sat down at a table, but she immediately got up and proceeded to have a chat with each person, and I sat there feeling a little neglected but conscious of a rising interest in her every move, until she finally resumed her "rightful" place at my side. We quickly turned our conversation to a more important subject: the feasibility of a late date after the dance.

Three years, three months, and twenty-eight days later, April 25, 1943, in the Methodist Church at Clarksdale, beneath the crossed sabres of six of my fraternity brothers, who were senior R.O.T.C. cadets at Ole Miss, and with shaking knees and tremulous voice, I married Nina Claire. At long last I heard the Reverend Shedhill Caffey verbally tie the knot by saying, "I now pronounce you man and wife."

After five days of driving across the vastness of the plains, mountains, and desert, we came into what seemed like a green wonderland of grass near San Luis Obispo. We stopped at a Mom and Pop country grocery store and bought eggs, bacon, butter, bread, coffee, and other necessities for our nesting place. We finally reached the beach house that I had rented in the village of

Cayucos, which was about five miles north of Morro Bay and about fifteen miles from my duty station.

The idea of leaving a wedding ceremony to drive five hundred miles each day for five days in order to report on time for duty after a leave of absence may fall a little short of what most people would like to have in the way of a honeymoon, but one must remember that this was wartime, and I felt a sense of accomplishment, or luck, to have been able to get a leave at all and to make it back to Oxford and Clarksdale to be married and then return on time to duty in California, all within about two weeks. I, of course, hoped for a little rest and respite for a day or so after getting back to Camp San Luis Obispo, but that was not to be.

The morning of my return to duty and for about three months thereafter, I had to get up at 5:00 A.M., drive the fifteen miles to the post, and report in before 7:00 A.M. I was responsible for getting my company to the many weapons ranges and having every member of the company trained to achieve an acceptable score in the target shooting.

Usually I would not get back home until after dark when the fog had rolled in and blanketed the last five miles along the beach road from Morro Bay to Cayucos. By then Nina would have reached a high state of apprehension which was increased when she learned from other officers' wives that their husbands had been getting home well before dark. She did not fully understand the difference in degrees of responsibility in being a staff officer and in being a separate unit commanding officer.

Saturday afternoons were sometimes free, and anticipation of their arrival was one of the bright thoughts which helped me through the weeks.

About two months after returning to Camp San Luis Obispo with my bride, I was able to get leave to be absent from Friday until Monday. Nina and I seized upon this occasion to go to Los Angeles and Hollywood. With some misgivings about leaving my unit when the "head hunters" were so active, I finally decided to take Nina to see the sights. I considered this trip more or less as a supplement to the honeymoon which had so far eluded us. We caught the Daylight Special at noon and felt a sense of release in getting away even for this short break in the demanding daily army routine.

In Los Angeles we got a room at the Ambassador Hotel. I had stayed there several times before and felt that I knew my way around. We shopped for razor blades and other items which were in short supply in wartime and which I would need while overseas. We made the usual tourist stops in Hollywood restaurants and saw a few movie stars. These were the heydays of the movie industry, and both Nina and I had, like most of our generation, been educated by movies about life in the world beyond Oxford, Clarksdale, and the Mid-South.

Scarcely a GI in the military service failed to have a favorite star from among Rita Hayworth, Ingrid Bergman, Lana Turner, or Dorothy Lamour. If the military had had an equal number of females as males, probably the pictures of Clark Gable, Robert Taylor, Spencer Tracy, and Cary Grant would have predominated as pinups. From Oxford a half dozen youngsters had migrated to Los Angeles after high school, presumably to be near the movie-making world.

I had heard that Mr. Billy had gotten a job as a writer with Warner Brothers. While sitting in our room at the Ambassador with Nina Claire and nearing the end of our weekend vacation in Los Angeles, I felt a twinge of homesickness for Oxford. I said to Nina Claire, "I know a fellow from Oxford named William Faulkner who is a writer. According to *The Oxford Eagle,* he is working here at one of the studios."

The name *William Faulkner* did not mean much, if anything to my bride of a couple of months. Although she was a recent graduate of Mississippi State College for Women, a highly accredited institution, she had not read Faulkner's novels. They were not part of most English curricula in Mississippi at that time. Not only did many Mississippians feel that the novelist denigrated his home state in his writings, but also throughout the country his career was in eclipse, with his work being out of print. Nina Claire had not read the worldly-wise and sometimes bizarre writings of William Faulkner.

Perhaps the faculty may have desired to shield the women from

69

the more revealing descriptions of the facts of life as Mr. Billy wrote of them. He sometimes suggested alternative views to the ideals of virtue, sobriety, virginity, and the holy estates of marriage and motherhood. Whatever may have been the reason, Nina was not familiar with Mr. Billy or his writings. She indicated, however, that since he was writing for the movie makers, she felt that he might be worth meeting when I had suggested calling on him.

When I telephoned Warner Brothers, Mr. Billy came on the line without much delay. We had a chat about Oxford and our families. It seemed to me that Mr. Billy was about as homesick as I. He invited us to come to his apartment later in the afternoon.

Nina Claire and I entered the foyer of the white stuccoed apartment building that was about a dozen floors in height. I felt some degree of uncertainty and timorousness about calling on Mr. Billy, whom I had not seen in many years. Soon after the button for his apartment was pressed, however, the elevator door opened, and out came Mr. Billy. He looked about the same as when I had last seen him. His moustache was a thin gray line above his lip and matched the gray of his hair. He wore a short-sleeved shirt and trousers, and appeared to have just returned from work.

I introduced Nina Claire to Mr. Billy as my recently acquired bride and filled him in about her education and having grown up in Clarksdale. We entered the elevator and went up to his apartment. He invited us out on the balcony from which could be seen much of the surrounding Hollywood area. Here and there a white high rise apartment or office building ascended about a dozen stories.

"How about a drink?" Mr. Billy asked and I quickly nodded my assent.

I did not glance at Nina Claire or even think of doing so to see if she approved. In Methodist, Baptist, and Presbyterian Sunday schools of bone-dry Mississippi, and particularly on the campus of the state's school for girls, the very thought of ladies' drinking alcoholic beverages was equated with desire to commit the cardinal sins. The "demon rum" was blamed for most misfortunes of mankind and even more so for those of womankind. Mississippi would remain a bone-dry state, at least for the record, for many years to come.

The girls had been discouraged from studies in human nature

and from the evils of cigarettes and alcohol by sharp-eyed house-mothers who had sniffed the breeze as the girls came in from dates or returned from a trip away from the campus. Despite these earlier attempts to frustrate her broader education, Nina was an apt pupil in learning the ways of army wives under the tutelage of some real masters of the art.

Mr. Billy went to fix the drinks with me at his side. He took some glasses from a shelf and a bottle from nearby. He didn't even use a jigger to measure the amount of liquor he poured into each drink; he just turned the bottle up and poured the glasses nearly full. Then he found some ice cubes and dropped one or two into each glass. Then we returned to the balcony.

Mr. Billy's bourbon had about as pretty a color as I had ever seen. It didn't even look like the PM and Three Feathers and Four Roses and such other brands of blended whiskey as usually could be found in liquor stores during World War II at prices which could be reached by a soldier's pay. I thought but did not say, This looks like the real Hollywood stuff.

While preparing to render a tasting test, I pulled out my pipe, thinking that in all of the libationary experiences in bars and officers' clubs and at private parties, and even in the Bachelor Officer's Quarters, I had never had a drink of straight whiskey such as this. Thus, I thought that a little smoke might fortify my system for this feat.

Mr. Billy noticed me stuffing my pipe by simply cramming the tobacco in the bowl and said, "Herman, I see you are smoking a pipe."

I said, "Yes sir, I got tired of trying to keep up with what I had done with lighted cigarettes and the pipe solved that problem."

Mr. Billy said, "Once I knew an old man who smoked a pipe. He took great care in stuffing his pipe. The old man would start loading his pipe by putting just a pinch of tobacco in the bottom of the bowl. Then he would carefully smooth the tobacco around the bottom. Then he would put a little more tobacco in and do the same thing, almost as if he were laying shingles on a roof. He would keep this up, just a little bit of tobacco each time, carefully spreading and leveling it around the bowl. After doing this as many times as necessary to fill the bowl up to about a quarter of an inch below the top of the bowl he would put his little finger in the bowl and gently tamp it down about another quarter of an inch.

"Finally, he would light a match and wait until it had burned away the smells and color of sulfur and the flame was exactly right and smelling only of burning wood, then he would move the match, now half-burned, around the bowl clockwise two or three times to be sure that the flame had lighted the tobacco evenly at every point in the bowl; and, as he circled the bowl with the match, he began to inhale just a little bit. He seemed to be merely breathing the smoke in and out instead of puffing and blowing. Puffing and blowing like a blacksmith's bellows would have made a ball of fire and overheated the pipe. The way he did it, the entire surface of the bowl let an even flow of smoke drift upward, and the fire could scarcely be seen. He kept on just sort of breathing the smoke in and out slowly and gently. After he got the pipe loaded and fired up, he could smoke that pipe on that load for four hours."

Nina and I had sat spellbound as Mr. Billy had unexpectedly launched into this extemporaneous lesson in how to load, light, and smoke a pipe. Ever afterwards, I would think of Mr. Billy's tale whenever I loaded and lit my own pipe. Yet, I was never able to so load and light and smoke my pipe that I could keep it going on a single loading for four hours.

By the end of that story, all three of us turned to our neglected glasses of bourbon and ice and found that the ice cubes had melted and thinned our drinks to a more drinkable mix.

As tongues touched the drinks the conversation became more relaxed. Nina Claire had loosened up considerably and found that although bourbon may promote vice and sin, it may also have the virtue of inspiring conversation. Suddenly Nina said: "Tell me, Mr. Billy, after being in Hollywood for quite a while, what is your impression of the place?"

Mr. Billy paused and looked at her. He took another sip from the vanishing bourbon in his glass, then he puffed on his pipe and looked out in the distance in the direction of the white stuccoed buildings near and far. He looked up at the sky, then at the mountains, and down toward the center of the city and said:

"I think of Hollywood as an alabaster city where nearly everything is phony and make-believe."

72

Chapter 6

The Intruder

In the summer of 1946 I returned to Oxford after about six years of military service before, during, and after World War II.

I got a job as adviser for veterans at Ole Miss and quickly became engrossed in the problems of the several thousand veterans who were attending the school. A year later I was also appointed supervisor of housing after my friend and classmate, William S. Griffin, resigned that position to become the first full-time alumni secretary the university had ever had. This too was a "hot spot" because there was so little housing available for faculty or students on the campus and in Oxford.

An air of excitement pervaded the town and campus as the rumors spread that a movie was going to be filmed in Oxford. It would be a version of Mr. Billy's latest book that no one seemed to have read, *Intruder in the Dust.*

When I first heard of this, I discounted such a possibility as unlikely. I was a member of the "movie generation," that is, the generation growing up in the period after the silent movies and before television, and it seemed to me that all movies, good, bad, or mediocre, were and should be filmed in far-off exotic places, not in a small Mississippi town like Oxford.

The first official notice I received was when I was called to a staff meeting by the university chancellor, Dr. John Davis Williams. He was flanked by Malcolm Guess, dean of men, and several other senior staff members. Obviously, something big was about to be considered.

As I sat there at the committee meeting, my thoughts drifted back to events that had transpired while I had served as supervisor of housing. My work had seldom been dull or routine in that position. There was the question of how strictly the traditional Ole Miss pre-war policy which banned the possession of transportation, drinking, or selling of alcoholic beverages on the campus, or the drinking of it elsewhere by Ole Miss students, should be enforced. Then there was the time when a student used the hallway of a dormitory as a pistol target range and fired his pistol down the hallway, endangering anyone who might come out of his room. Once the traditional Law Day celebration by the law students erupted into a brawl. Perhaps the most interesting story, however, was that of "Popcorn Annie."

In October, a popcorn machine had been installed in the Student Union Building near the post office. Almost every member of the campus population went to the post office one or more times daily. The aroma of popping corn spread throughout the building and even was discernible outside the building. A very pretty young lady was employed to cook and sell the popcorn.

Business was brisk. She made many acquaintances, especially among the younger male students. Soon rumors began to filter up to the offices of the Lyceum that Annie was diversifying her activities; that while she was selling popcorn by day, she was favoring her many friends with her personal charms in the men's dormitories at night; the latter being a non-commercial undertaking done only for fun and recreation.

Anything as sensational as a resident dispenser of sex in the dormitories could not long remain a secret. An investigation revealed that there was truth in the rumors. Obviously, something had to be done.

A considerable number of male university students were discovered to have been involved with Popcorn Annie at the popcorn machine by day and in the men's dormitory rooms by night. In short order, the pattern emerged as one after another admitted that he had eaten popcorn at Annie's stand and taken his turn in bedding Annie by night. Various estimates of the number of students who had nocturnal experiences with Annie were reported as approximately fifty the first night, forty the second night, and thirty the third night. Obviously, the novelty was wearing thin or the demand had been satisfied.

The affair took on a more serious note when questions were raised about the age of Annie, for it seemed that she was somewhere around sixteen or seventeen years of age, the difference being whether this might be a criminal offense of a capital degree in Mississippi since the state had a statute stipulating sexual intercourse with a female of sixteen years or younger as "statutory rape," and rape could be punishable by death. Inquiry as to criminal conduct was the business of the courts—not college officials.

Several of the students were required to "withdraw" from the university for a semester or so. Annie was not seen around the campus any more, and the popcorn business was closed down.

In early December when I got to the office there was a whispering and giggling going on among the secretarial staff. Naturally I asked what was going on, what was the subject for the morning, what was it that they knew that I did not know?

At this point the senior secretary brought me a copy of a newspaper from a distant city. In a prominent place in the paper, maybe on the front page of the second section, there was a picture of a chorus which would sing and perform in the forthcoming Christmas pageant. In the front row of the chorus of "angels" was none other than Popcorn Annie.

Yet another chapter would occur for events such as this had been were slow to completely disappear and be forgotten. The following year the Ole Miss versus Mississippi State football game was played on the Ole Miss campus. The game was then played every other year on the home campus of each of Mississippi's major universities. As usual, the game was anticipated with mounting interest as the time in late November drew near. Usually this game had a bearing on the championship of the Southeastern Conference of which both universities were members. The stadium was filled to overflowing by around 35,000 fans. At half time the band of each school played and paraded and put on an extravaganza of drilling in precise formations. The drum majorettes, scantily clad in shiny sequinned costumes, had finished their twirling and dancing routines. The activities on the field reached the state of anticlimatic pause. At this precise point in time, a single student walked on the track which surrounded the football field. He came from the Mississippi State side of the field near the southeast corner of the stadium. He carried a large sign which was fastened to a pole, somewhat like the color bearers had carried, and the sign extended up to about twelve feet in the air. The contents of the sign could not be seen from the Ole Miss side of the stadium. As he walked north in front of the Mississippi State stand, a peculiar roar commenced, then expanded into a crescendo as he walked along. It was not like the usual noises of cheers of football fans. Rather, it seemed to be something like about twenty thousand people laughing uncontrollably.

As the sign bearer progressed to the north end of the east side stands, he sauntered unhurriedly around the circling track at the north end of the stadium and finally came into view of the Ole Miss fans. There a different reaction was encountered. It seemed as though that crowd of fans were stricken with embarrassment and low-pitched boos and muffled curses could be heard. The man behind me said, "Those dirty sons of bitches." Words of like import came from many others when they saw the sign. It read:

Sheriff's Sale
One Popcorn Machine

As my thoughts returned to the matters at hand—the filming of *Intruder in the Dust*—I noticed there was present at the meeting a man with a camera case hanging from his shoulder. He was an advance man for the movie-making company, and he wanted to know whether it might be possible for the movie colony to be housed on campus and what facilities the university could make available to the movie makers.

There seemed to me to be a bit of coolness to the proposition by the chancellor and, since he was the chief executive of the university, the other high officials, like good staffers everywhere, detected and reflected his attitude and fell in line, as staffers usually do. They listened with a sort of strained politeness. I thought that they did not seem very interested in aiding the visitor's cause at all. Someone asked me if it would be feasible for the university to provide housing for the movie colony. Attempting to leave some room for maneuvering, I said, "It might be possible under certain conditions." I was thinking of seasonal vacancies, but I quickly sensed from raised eyebrows and exchanges of glances that I had not said what the other officials wanted to hear or what was expected of me. I had difficulty in trying to figure out exactly what my seniors may have wanted to hear, or by what subliminal method it had been communicated among them that the university did not wish to become involved in the production of a movie based upon a novel written by William Faulkner. The meeting dragged on.

The advance man then wanted to know what famous alumni Ole Miss had produced. The chancellor was relatively new and knew few, if any, of such famous people as would be of interest to a movie maker. Dean Guess had been on the campus for many years, and it seemed to me that he should have known any celebrities which the school had produced, but he did not come forth with any such information.

Again the chancellor's finger pointed at me, and he said, "You are a fairly recent graduate and in charge of veterans and housing, surely you must know what he wants to hear."

Around the Ole Miss campus the chancellor represents the summit of power. Thus, driven by the desire to please, I frantically tried to think of some truly outstanding alumnus but to no avail. I could feel myself on a free fall from official favor. I had been away from the campus for about six years during World War II. Although I had grown up in Oxford and had followed the careers of a few graduates and my personal heroes, they were mainly of football fame, such as great All-Americans like Bruiser Kinard and Buster Poole, or a dance band leader, or friends who had attained above average rank or won a decoration in the military during World War II. None seemed to deserve classification as a "celebrity." No truly famous Ole Miss graduate's name came to my mind. I did consider, but then rejected, the names of certain politicians, senators, governors, judges, and the like, figuring that Ole Miss might be better off with their names forgotten, or at least not publicized. All I could safely do was to mention the All-American football players who came to mind. These names did not favorably impress the advance man or the chancellor.

I did recall that the most famous person having an Ole Miss affiliation was the author of the book soon to be made into a movie, which was the reason for the meeting. I realized however, that Mr. Billy was best remembered as having sold stamps to the campus population and having shoveled coal to keep the buildings warm and lighted. Mr. Billy was not really a "graduated" alumnus of Ole Miss although he had attended the university, more or less, for a semester or so. I thought it best to hold my tongue about such things. The exact position and stature which William Faulkner was to occupy in the hierarchy of Ole Miss values had not yet been determined. There was no bust of him in the library. He had not yet received the Nobel Prize for his contribution to literature.

The meeting ended upon a flattened note with promises that the university would do some studies and try to determine who the more famous Ole Miss sons and daughters might be. I remembered the alma mater's prayer-like words: "May her fame throughout the nation through her sons and daughters grow."

There had been the perfect opportunity for a little bragging and some good public relations for Ole Miss, but I felt that I had fumbled and lost the ball and failed to score. As to the housing of the movie makers, I experienced some puzzlement. Why was the official attitude of the university one of opposition to the housing of the movie colony on the campus?

I later learned that some reticence was felt by the senior officials concerning the propriety of the university being a party to filming a book by William Faulkner. Mr. Billy had sometimes written of whorehouses, an idiot in love with a cow, and the deteriorating southern aristocracy. I recalled a political hullabaloo and a legislative investigation which had once occurred because some book was placed in the library which dealt with the breeding of black and white rabbits. It offended the tender sensibilities of some, including politicians who could seize upon such a controversy to start a crusade against suggestions for change in the southern "traditions" if they touched by innuendo upon racial integration or miscegenation, particularly if it appeared that state-supported institutions might be promoting such ideas. If legislators could find a basis for suspicion of advocacy of intermixing black and white, be it of rabbits or people, within the state university, their political future would be enhanced. If some "liberal" faculty or staff member at the state university could be found at fault, the institution would pay a heavy price.

There also seemed to have been some genuine doubt among the university officials as to the wisdom of lending the facilities of the state university in aid of a purely commercial venture like the filming of a movie for the profit of Hollywood and Mr. Billy.

I, too, wondered as to the propriety of such an undertaking after thinking of some of the more sensational plots and descriptions Mr. Billy had authored in portions of *Sanctuary,* the first of his books to gain him notoriety and prove profitable to him. It was the most violent of his novels. In it the rape of an Ole Miss coed named Temple Drake with a corn cob caused Mr. Billy sometimes to be referred to as "the corn cob man."

I speculated that this may have caused some officials to be reluctant to assume any responsibility for the use of university facilities in producing a movie based upon any of Mr. Billy's books. Indeed, there were lots of Mississippians who had not yet been convinced of the high position in the literary world which Mr. Billy had attained. They surely would have doubted that one day at the approaches to the city there would be a huge sign reading, "Welcome to Oxford—Home of William Faulkner," or that his bust would stand in the library of the university.

Thus it was that the members of the movie colony were left to find lodging in the two small local hotels or in boarding houses or wherever they could.

Soon the actors, crew, directors, and officials came in surprising numbers, and filming got under way. Townspeople became accustomed to seeing actors, whom they had seen on the movie

79

screens of the town's two theaters, sitting near them in a local restaurant. It was almost like the attraction Hollywood restaurants had been to the GIs in World War II. In the Brown Derby restaurant, I once had lunched at a table next to one occupied by the glamorous actress, Dorothy Lamour. In pre-World War II movies, dressed in a sarong and with flowers in her hair, she had given a vastly different impression of what life was like in the South Pacific islands from that which GIs actually found.

In making the movie in Oxford, certain scenes, particularly mob scenes, required several hundred people to participate, and many townspeople enrolled to play a part. The pay was something near the minimum wage of that day.

As filming got under way, much of the activity occurred near the home of my mother on Johnson Avenue, which runs east from South Lamar and down through a little valley or "hollow." Because it had no curbs, gutters, or pavement, it looked like a country road.

For several weeks the camera crews with lights of every kind, brightness, and color were at work at night in the street. From that intersection eastward to South 13th Street through the hollow, it appeared to me that some very important scene was being enacted and re-enacted many times.

A strange looking, tall, shaggy, graying, long-eared mule, unlike any local mule I had ever seen, was a principal performer. At a given signal, he would charge at breakneck speed down the sloping street. A boy of early teenage years rode on the mule, clutching the animal's neck as his body bounced up and down and his legs flopped about from side to side. It appeared as though the mule was going to run for a great distance, but after 150 feet of this reckless dash, the mule would slow down, stop, and amble back at a leisurely mulelike pace to the starting point to await the order to do it all over again. Sometimes this scene was done in the daylight, then again at night, over and over again. It appeared that the director was trying for perfection in this scene.

At night, floodlights blazed and cast dark shadows along the valley street and created the appearance of mule and boy dashing frantically down a country lane. Their purpose was to let the sheriff know of the impending lynch mob action in order to save the life of the innocent Negro who was suspected of a murder. The scene made me think of the midnight ride of Paul Revere as he hastened to alarm the colonists that the British were coming.

Again and again the scene was re-enacted. First, it was done in daylight, which doubtlessly had proven unsatisfactory. Somewhat later the nighttime filming continued with alternate discontinuances and resumptions over a period of months. Once when I was watching the activity, the mule, while returning from one of his gallops, looked me right in the eyes with what seemed to me a level of intelligence exceeding that of many humans. I imagined the mule to be thinking that so much repetition of the scene was becoming a little silly, but was a requirement of being a movie star.

Several years later I saw the finished movie. I had assumed that all of the painstaking effort given to this scene would make it a very important part, perhaps the climactic point, in the finished film. I was a little disappointed to find that this protracted and

Photo courtesy of Herman E. Taylor

The Stowers-Longest Home
This home on the corner of South Lamar Boulevard and Johnson Avenue was used as the home of Gavin Stevens in the film *Intruder in the Dust.* Johnson Avenue was the site of the "mule scene."

diligent effort by the film colony in this episode consumed no more than a few seconds in the finished version of the movie.

Half a block north along South Lamar from its intersection with Johnson Avenue another scene was filmed. It caught my attention off and on as I passed along on the way to and from the square. It occurred near the hedge along the sidewalk of the J. E. Neilson home, a stately old gray frame house which had been built around 1835 by John D. Martin. A two-story house, square in shape with windows extending from the floor to the ceiling of the lower level, it was painted a leadish shade of gray. Above the first floor level, the walls sloped upward toward the center of the house on all sides. It had a large banistered porch where at times Mr. and Mrs. Neilson sat and surveyed the neighborhood.

The movie makers began work on another scene on the west side of the Neilson's front yard. In the scene filmed there, the former mayor of Oxford, Robert X. Williams, played the part of the owner of the home. Bob Williams had married Mr. Billy's first cousin, Sallie Murry Wilkins. I surmised that this possibly accounted for Mr. Bob's role as an actor in the movie.

During all of my childhood and teenage years, Mr. Williams, a native of Taylor, Mississippi, was of particular importance to me because he operated the Lyric Theater and personally sold the tickets. A time or two Mr. Williams had let me deliver circulars around the square and town to announce some special showing, or just to drum up trade, all for the price of a "free" admission for me to see a movie. Usually the price was twenty-five cents for the matinee and night showing but only a dime for the Saturday afternoon western cowboy shows.

Years later as I watched the movie, and this scene in particular, I was impressed with the words Mr. Billy had spoken to me as we talked on his balcony in Hollywood. Mr. Billy had said that all in Hollywood was "phony and make-believe." This recollection was prompted by the voice of Mr. Williams when I finally saw the movie. Mr. Williams had said, "There is going to be a necktie party tonight."

To my dismay in watching the movie, when the scene reached the place where Mr. Williams spoke, the voice which came out of his mouth was not his voice at all. It was a high-pitched voice of someone else dubbed in to suit the imagination of some movie director as to what an Oxford voice should sound like.

I felt a little resentful at the implication that leading citizens of Oxford would have participated directly, or indirectly, in a lynching—even by circulating the message that a lynch mob was planning some action.

I found myself disenchanted with the phoniness of the Hollywood approach and what I believed a misrepresentation of the people of my hometown. On the other hand, I remembered that Oxford was Mr. Billy's hometown, too, and that lynchings had occurred in Oxford in 1908 and during the 1930s.

In several of Mr. Billy's novels, he had mentioned lynching, or near lynchings. In *Sanctuary,* published in 1930, he had described the lynching by "gasoline and flame" of Lee Goodwin. Goodwin was charged with the murder of a white man and accused of the corn cob rape of Temple Drake. Because of the perjury of Temple at the trial, it appeared that Goodwin was guilty of both crimes. While this was not true, an outraged community took the law into its own hands.

In 1932, Faulkner described the killing of Joe Christmas by Percy Grimm after Joe had escaped while en route to his trial, and how Joe was castrated by Percy after being fatally wounded. In *Intruder in the Dust,* a lynching of a Negro suspected of killing a white man, who was actually killed by a white man, was narrowly averted by the courage of a determined sheriff.

Some analogies may be drawn between these events and actual events which had occurred in or near Oxford in earlier years. When William Faulkner was at the impressionable age of eleven, Nelse Patton, a Negro, was arrested for the murder of a white woman with a straight-edge razor in an apparent attempt to rape her. He was lodged in the Lafayette County Jail. On September 8, 1908, a mob broke into the jail and killed him, then mutilated him by castration. I was told that Nelse was killed in the jail when he was struck in the head with a pick axe, and that the skin of the scalp was pulled down over his face. Then his body was dragged behind a car to the south entrance of the courthouse, and there hanged naked from a large oak tree which stood to the west side of the sidewalk between the courthouse and the Confederate monument. These events were substantiated by a newspaper report held by the Mississippi Department of Archives and History and by eyewitnesses.

Around 1930, a Negro who was accused of raping a white woman in the Etta Community of Union County, a few miles from what would later become Mr. Billy's farm, Greenfield, was reportedly tortured and emasculated, then burned to death while a huge crowd looked on.

Such was part of the Oxford and Lafayette County environment of which Mr. Billy wrote. These stories I had heard of lynch mob actions taken by the local people seemed to have played an important part in providing some of the inspiration of Mr. Billy's recurring themes.

Intruder in the Dust also depicted the legal environment of the period. It was a time when civil rights legislation in Congress was customarily met by Senate filibuster. It was before the U.S. Supreme Court decision of 1962 in *Baker vs. Carr* which decreed "one man one vote" and changed the political power structure of America, particularly that of the South.

It was before the Civil Rights Act of 1964. Before this act, the plight of the southern black had been somewhat like the plight of the peasant of Central Europe before the nineteenth century revolutions sent tyrants to their doom and gave to the poor, the uneducated, and the politically powerless in those societies the possibility of becoming economically strong and politically powerful, or at least the possibility of shedding the burdens of their heredity. For more than a century after the Civil War, the battle would continue between those for and against civil rights for blacks.

The filming of *Intruder in the Dust* dragged on and on, in and around the town and county, from rural roads and scenes to the courthouse square and the county jail.

At times, the needs of the movie makers became something of a minor annoyance to local business people and those who found traffic routed around some filming site. Several scenes were to be shot on the square, the hub of Oxford's business. The movie mak-

The Old Jail
The Lafayette County Jail was an important feature in many of Faulkner's novels, and was described in detail in *Requiem for a Nun.* The jailer's family lived on the first floor and the prisoners occupied the second floor.

ing activities posed a special problem in that it would interfere with the work of the community if done on a business day.

To minimize the disruption of business, some of the filming was done on Sunday afternoon, the usual low point of activity on and around the square.

On one Sunday afternoon, I went up to the square to watch the goings on. I stood in front of Avent's Drug Store near the northwestern corner of the square, where a scene was being filmed.

An old, mud-splattered, brown four-door automobile charged onto the vacated west half of the square from South Lamar. It lurched and rocked along at a rapid speed. One of its tires was flat and it flopped, as though recently blown out. With a screeching of brakes and tires, it swerved from side to side. It came to a jerking halt near Patton's Barber Shop. The sheriff in the movie, whose real name was Will Geer, had brought in the Negro man who was suspected of having committed murder. In the final movie version this was depicted as the sheriff's arrival at the jail. Actually, the jail was about two blocks away from the barber shop.

In a later scene, which actually was made in front of the jail, the sheriff confronted the assembled mob of a couple of hundred and told them, "There ain't going to be any lynching," and bluffed them out of any such attempt. He got the suspect safely into the jail. That mob scene in front of the jail was the suspenseful high point of the film.

As I watched the activities on the square that Sunday afternoon, I recalled that I was standing in front of what had been the Kroger grocery store in the 1930s. I had worked there for several years in the afternoons and on Saturdays, and there by the curb was where I had last seen Miss Estelle, Mr. Billy's wife.

On one occasion while working there, the telephone had rung, and Miss Estelle was on the line. She wanted to know if she could give me the grocery order and have me fill it and bring it out to her car when she came by to pick up the groceries. I said I could and would. After a time she appeared with her Negro driver driving the car. I carried the groceries out to her car, being pleased to have the opportunity to see her for the first time in several years. I also hoped to glean a bit of information about Cho Cho while delivering the groceries.

Miss Estelle, in the accustomed manner of great ladies, had waited in the car to be waited on. She was dressed as if going to some social event in the diplomatic corps. Her voice made a pleasant purring sound which caused my sense of values to classify her as a "high class lady." She even had on white gloves that extended somewhere above her wrists. Her hair came down softly over her ears and toward the front of her cheekbones.

She had greeted me warmly, although she had not seen me since Cho Cho's last party at Rowan Oak. She even paid me some compliment about how tall I had grown, which made me feel very good about myself. I thought that this was a mark of a truly great lady who could make even a grocery clerk feel important.

I put the sack of groceries in the car, accepted her money, ran back in for change, returned, and stood there at the curb admiringly as I watched her being driven away.

Now I was watching the sheriff's old car finish its noisy approach. Out of the periphery of my vision, I saw a man standing in the recessed entrance to the stairs leading to offices above Avent's Drug Store. He was watching, as was I, the movie-making activities. The man had on a floppy hat with brim turned down all around, a tweedy-looking coat, and baggy flannel trousers. He had a moustache above his lips and a pipe in his mouth. There stood Mr. Billy!

I had not seen him in the several years since we visited on his balcony in Hollywood, despite the fact that we both had been in Oxford for two or three years since the end of World War II. Mr. Billy had been in and out of town, and I had been fully occupied in becoming re-civilianized since my return from military service in 1946.

In a small town most people form a pattern of activities in their daily and yearly routines, and it is not unusual for years to pass without their seeing one another, unless they wish to do so, or some common interest causes their trails to cross. Not seeing Mr. Billy was not unusual. He ordinarily kept to himself and took little or no part in civic or social activities, while staying close to his home. He occasionally did take up some cause in which he was interested and when he did so, he had a considerable ability to influence action through his writings.

Once, Mr. Billy published an item in *The Oxford Eagle*, the local weekly newspaper and the chief means of learning what was going on in the town and county. He condemned projected plans for demolition of the old courthouse. The writing was effective.

William Faulkner Made Effort to Save Courthouse

Bravo your piece about the preservation of the courthouse. I am afraid your cause is already lost though. We have gotten rid of the shade trees which once circled the courthouse yard and bordered the Square itself, along with the second floor galleries which once formed awnings for the sidewalk; all we have left now to distinguish an old southern town from any one of ten thousand towns built

Photo courtesy of Jack Cofield

The Lafayette County Courthouse
The courthouse was built in 1842, partly destroyed by Yankee troops in 1864, rebuilt in 1872, enlarged with east and west wings in 1952, and renovated and modernized about 1980.

yesterday from Kansas to California are the Confederate monument, the courthouse and the jail. Let us tear them down too and put up something covered with neon and radio amplifiers.

Your cause is doomed. They will go the way of the old Cumberland church. It was here in 1861; it was the only building on or near the square still standing in 1865. It was tougher than war, tougher than the Yankee Brigadier Chalmers and his artillery and all his sappers with dynamite and crowbars and cans of kerosene. But it wasn't tougher than the ringing of a cash register bell. It had to go—obliterated, effaced, no trace left—so that a sprawling octopus covering the country from Portland, Maine to Oregon can dispense in cut-rate bargain lots, bananas and toilet paper.

They call this progress. But they don't say where it's going; also there are some of us who would like the chance to say whether or not we want the ride.

—William Faulkner*

*Reprinted from *The Oxford Eagle,* March 13, 1947

88

The Lafayette County Courthouse After 1952
Faulkner's writings helped prevent the demolition of the courthouse in 1947. A plaque at the south entrance features a quotation from *Requiem for a Nun* in which he praised the architecture and history of the courthouse.

Photo courtesy of Herman E. Taylor

The county officials abandoned plans for demolishing the courthouse, and instead modernized and expanded the original structure with wings to the east and west to provide better accommodations for county offices and courts.

As I advanced to greet him, Mr. Billy seemed genuinely pleased to see me and shook my hand warmly. We chatted briefly about how the fates had brought us both back home to Oxford. Just as we greeted each other, the overwhelming sound of the ringing of the town clock atop the courthouse drowned out our conversation.

Later on, I speculated that it may have been about this time that Mr. Billy was working on his novel *Requiem for a Nun.* In that novel he wrote an exhaustive description, however fictional or authoritative, of the origins and construction of the courthouse and the jail. I guessed that the local controversy over replacing the old courthouse may have inspired Mr. Billy to have written of the courthouse in that book, which was published in 1951. He described how in 1864 Yankee troops under Major General A. J. Smith had been successful in burning out the inside woodwork, but unsuccessful in the attempted demolition of the columned entrances.

I remarked to Mr. Billy that it was a great accomplishment for his book to be made into a movie right here at home. He seemed pleased. He said that it was good to have the movie filmed in Oxford because, "It has provided a lot of jobs for the local people and some business for the town." I could not have then imagined that six years later my recollection of those words would infuriate Mr. Billy and force me to re-evaluate his interest in the well-being of our hometown and county.

By then some of the action around the old car featured in the movie scene caught our attention, and we drifted apart in the gathering crowd.

Soon the filming was finished, and the movie colony gradually diminished in size and activities and no longer intruded in the town and county.

Reflections

Chapter 7

Names

Is there anything of great importance in the spelling of a family's name?

Should Falkners reject, or adopt, the *Faulkner* spelling of the family's name? The Falkners were proud of the Falkner name and proud of the given names of their ancestors. The main road from Oxford to New Albany, Mississippi, was named Falkner Highway. There is a town in North Mississippi near the Tennessee state boundary named Falkner. Some Falkner ancestors of Mr. Billy gained prominence in their careers.

Mr. Billy's great-grandfather, William Clark Falkner, sometimes called "the Old Colonel," was an officer in the Confederate Army, a railroad builder, and an author. Mr. Billy's grandfather, John Wesley Thompson Falkner, sometimes called "the Young Colonel," was a bank president and a lawyer in Oxford. Mr. Billy's uncle, John Wesley Thompson Falkner, Jr., was also a lawyer, and was called Uncle John by Johncy Falkner in his book, *My Brother Bill.* Johncy was Mr. Billy's brother, whose real name was John Wesley Thompson Falkner III. The son of Uncle John was named John Wesley Thompson Falkner IV, but he was called John, Jr.

I wondered why Mr. Billy had changed the spelling of his family's name. It seemed doubtful to me that any relative of mine would approve of, or emulate, any family member changing the spelling of our family name. However, I concluded that a man's name is his own to keep or change at will, in honor or disgrace.

To my way of thinking, there was something wrong with changing the spelling of the family name by a single member of a family. I acknowledged, however, that there would always be those situations where an individual, having disgraced himself and his family name, would be encouraged by family members to change his surname. If, on the other hand, he should gain great and favorable acclaim, it would seem to deprive the family of its right to a share in the reflected glory if he rejected the family name. Such a change of name might require all of his relatives to explain that, despite his change of the family name, he really is their kin. It might also provide incentive for adopting for themselves the name change in order to benefit from any fame. The problems would be simplified if a complete change of name were made as from *Smith* to *Brown.* Where, however, the change is of but a single letter, as by inserting a *u* in the Falkner name, the new name is too much like the former name to be disassociated from it. Yet *Faulkner* from *Falkner* is not so different as to be entirely new and separable for it is inescapably related but distinguishable and distinctive.

For reasons of anonymity, vanity, self laudation, or otherwise, persons and the fictitious beings which are called corporations are usually free to call themselves whatever they may please, and many authors, like movie actors, have adopted a pseudonym by which to be known, as if it were a trademark.

Had I considered the matter before it happened, I would have thought it highly unlikely that I would have ever become embroiled in a controversy over the spelling of any family's name, but I was about to discover the perversity of such involvement with none other than Mr. Billy's Uncle John, John W. T. Falkner, attorney at law, Oxford, Mississippi.

Upon the passing of "General" James Stone, Oxford's most prominent lawyer and father of Mr. Billy's close friend, Phil Stone, Uncle John succeeded to the top position among lawyers in the town and county. In nearly every small town in Mississippi, particularly if it is the county seat, one lawyer seems to lead the pack. More frequently than not, he has the business of the establishment, carries great influence in political affairs, is a member of the board of directors of the bank, quite possibly serves as counsel of the board of supervisors, and has a clientele which sometimes includes the most influential people in the town. His views are sought upon most everything, legal or otherwise, and his opinions, curbstone or in writing, are widely quoted as authority or justification for whatever might be in question within the broad scope of human affairs.

Mr. Billy's Uncle John was counsel for the First National Bank of Oxford. He had an office on a floor above the bank. The entrance to his office was about fifty feet from the corner of North Lamar Boulevard and the square, and the office could be reached by a narrow winding stairway entered from the sidewalk on the west side of the street. There was a window in an interior wall in his office which overlooked the main floor of the bank. This, in my imagination, was the bank which inspired one of Mr. Billy's novels, *Sartoris,* in which the bookkeeper, Byron Snopes, embezzled some money and fled the town of Jefferson.

After the death of my father, Guy B. Taylor, my mother had turned to Mr. Falkner for such legal services as she might need, and she thought that he was the smartest lawyer to be found. In natural course, as I grew up, I also consulted Uncle John when I found myself upon the verge of a legal controversy.

My first legal problem confronted me at the age of eighteen when a musician in my dance band, The Ole Miss Collegians, quit my band and joined a competing band.

I climbed the narrow spiraling stairs to the office above the bank to consult with Mr. Falkner. This would be the first of many lessons in the practice of law which I would receive from Uncle John.

Mr. Falkner said, "Yes, that contract seems reasonable and proper, but the piano player is a minor and cannot be made to abide by his contract. Further, you cannot enforce a contract by specific performance for services of an artistic nature."

I said, "Do you mean that I can't do anything?"

Mr. Falkner replied, "You might be able to get an injunction to keep him from playing with anyone else."

"What's that you said?" I asked.

Mr. Falkner continued, "You would have to post a bond of five hundred dollars as a condition to filing suit for an injunction."

Now in that day and circumstance, one could attend Ole Miss for an entire school year for five hundred dollars. That would include the tuition of one hundred dollars and leave enough money for the year's room and board. That was the amount I hoped to earn, at least in part, by managing the band.

Obviously, this matter had gotten out of hand on economic grounds.

"Maybe I had better think that over," I said as Mr. Falkner nodded approvingly. I had had my first lesson in the field of law and the subjects of Contracts and Equity Jurisprudence. I decided, upon nonlegal grounds, that it would be better to find another piano player.

In the years after my return to Oxford from World War II and before being recalled to active duty in the Korean conflict, I earned a degree from the Ole Miss Law School. Completion of the last semester was made possible by a two months' extension of the time for reporting for active duty, granted by the army.

During the period "between wars," I had become interested in real estate in Oxford and hoped to acquire as much of it as possible. Next door to my mother's three-acre lot and pasture was a lot of approximately the same size which was owned by Mrs. A. E. Hickey, the widow of the town's blacksmith.

There were about two acres of her lot which had grown up in weeds and brush since Mr. Hickey's death. All outbuildings were in disrepair. The property was on a hillside sloping to the west. I thought that this land would make good building sites, if ever the unopened portion of South 14th Street should be opened, graded, and paved.

With this in mind, I approached Mrs. Hickey to see if I might arrange to purchase this part of her pasture. I offered her twelve hundred dollars for the land. To my surprise, she was willing to sell it immediately. She told me to get the necessary papers readied. This I did and went back to see her that afternoon. When I returned a few hours later, to my dismay, she said, "I have sold the land to Mr. Falkner."

Seeing my astonishment she added, "I called to ask him about your offer and he said, 'Why, I will pay you fifteen hundred dollars for that land,' so I sold it to him."

I was learning things about the practice of law not taught in schools of law.

A year or so later my older brother, Guy B., and I undertook to have the land behind our mother's house, once used as a pasture, subdivided into residential lots fronting on South 14th Street. There was a strip of land a few feet wide and approximately five hundred feet long on the east side of the right of way between our mother's pasture fence, which served as her property line, and the land Mr. Falkner had bought from Mrs. Hickey.

Sometime after South 14th Street was graded, curbed, paved with asphalt, and opened for use, Guy called me at my army station in Philadelphia, Pennsylvania, and said that a problem had arisen regarding the boundary of the adjoining properties and that Mr. Falkner had removed the pasture fence. It seemed to me and my brother that something should be done, but what?

After an extended period of brooding and researching the law and the facts, I concluded that I should at least write Mr. Falkner to inquire as to his actions, and to give him a chance to explain or offer to make a token payment as consideration for the land in order to clarify the title and the boundary line. Accordingly, I wrote him a letter, intending to open negotiations toward an amicable settlement of the matter. Without giving the spelling of his name so much as a single thought, I addressed the letter as follows:

> Honorable John W. T. Faulkner
> Attorney at Law
> Oxford, Mississippi

A week or so after the letter was sent, my secretary came into my office with a puzzled expression on her face and remarked, "Here is a strange letter, which may be for you, but I can't be sure."

"What's that?" I said to Frances. "What do you mean?"

"Well, it has your rank, first name and middle initial on it, but the last name surely is not yours."

Reaching for the letter, I replied, "Now Frances, what are you talking about? Let's see."

She handed me the letter which was addressed, Lt. Colonel Herman E. Tailer.

I noted that the letter had come from Oxford, Mississippi, and bore the return address of "John W. T. Falkner, Attorney at Law."

It did not occur to me, as I opened the envelope, that the misspelling of my own name in the address had been other than unintentional.

Inside the envelope, the address on the correspondence was the same. Remembering that Mr. Falkner had never had a secretary, I assumed that he had typed the letter himself and had made a typographical error. It bore none of the finesse with which a professional secretary might type a letter. I knew that Mr. Falkner was getting older and thought that he might merely have hit the wrong keys, then had failed to proofread his copy. I did think it strange that he would make such an error on both the envelope and in the letter.

The letter did not contain a word relating to the matter about which I had written to Mr. Falkner, that is, his removal of the fence on the east side of South 14th Street. Instead, it read:

> Dear Colonel Tailer:
> As long as you have known me and my family I should think that you would be aware of the correct spelling of my name.

I suddenly realized that the misspelling of my own name had not been due to error or oversight. After pondering the meaning of this letter, I had a feeling that it contained some message which was overly subtle and obscure.

The next morning I awoke and felt relieved because my introspection had shed some light upon Mr. Falkner's enigmatic subterfuge. Upon analysis it appeared very clear to me that Uncle John did not care for Mr. Billy's innovativeness, that of inserting a *u* into the Falkner name. The letter as a whole seemed to me to be nothing more than a fogging of the issues. Yet I found myself empathizing with Uncle John's frustration with his nephew's perversion of a proud family name. The resulting *Faulkner* name could scarcely be disassociated from the Falkner name. Might the tidal wave of Mr. Billy's fame induce the Falkner progeny eventually to adopt the *Faulkner* spelling?

Mr. Falkner's letter appeared to be a tactic to divert attention from the real, or the substantive issue, as lawyers have often done. It had changed the nature of the correspondence from a consideration of the legal matter complained of to an issue over the spelling of his family name.

Then I recalled Mr. Falkner's letter and gloatingly said to myself, And there's not a damned thing he can do about that *u* in the Falkner name. . . .

Now understanding the game better, I wrote in reply:

> Dear Mr. Falkner:
> At the time I wrote to you concerning your removal of our fence, which subject you ignored in your reply, I was completely unaware of the controversy within your family over the proper spelling of your family name. I was aware that a very famous relative of yours spells his name FAULKNER.

Improvisation in the spelling of the names of people and places was one of Mr. Billy's writing skills. According to the book *A Faulkner Glossary* by Harry Runyan, the Chickasaw Indians spelled the river's name *Yocona petopha,* the Indian name meaning "split land." Mr. Billy combined these words and with variations thereupon named the county which was the centerpiece of his storytelling Yoknapatawpha. His allusions, hints, and innuendos in referring to actual places by fictional names are as inescapable as they are distinctive. When reading one of Mr. Billy's books, those who know his town and county and their people continually ask themselves the questions: Was he writing about me or someone or some place I know? Was White Leaf Creek alluding to Yellow Leaf Creek? Was Frenchman's Bend depicting the village of Taylor, Fudgetown, Yocona, Tula, or a synthesis of all of them? When writing of one's own habitat, deceptive names for people and places of a fictitious town or county could protect the author from libel suits while creating and proliferating mysteries.

In the summer of 1985, Nina Claire and I went to Oxford and

Photo courtesy of Herman E. Taylor

The Valley of the Yocona River
The Chickasaw Indians called the Yocona River *Yocona petopha,* which means "split land." Faulkner derived "Yoknapatawpha" from these words describing the river which flows near the southern border of Lafayette County.

Ole Miss to attend the Faulkner and Yoknapatawpha Conference and to hear what the experts from Russia, France, Japan, the North, South, West, and East might know about Mr. Billy that we did not know. I believed that these scholars might be more knowledgeable of Mr. Billy's writings than I was.

One tour took the visitors to the Episcopal church in Oxford. I had been inside this church only a few times in the process of growing up. A stained glass window on the north side of the church became the center of the group's attention. Unlike their Uncle John, who was a staunch Methodist, Mr. Billy and Miss Estelle, Johncy and his wife, Lucile Ramey Falkner, were Episcopalians. The stained glass window had been installed in memory of Johncy, who was John Wesley Thompson Falkner III, but in the name there was something which caught the attention of everyone present. In his name there had been inserted the letter *u* in parenthesis after the *a,* making his name read John Wesley Thompson Fa(u)lkner III. Mr. Billy's innovation in the family name had spread laterally among his kin and was being perpetuated. At the seminars of the Faulkner Festival, the sons of Johncy and Lucile Falkner, Jimmy and Chooky, were on the program. They had been friends of mine since childhood. Each had a part on the program to answer questions and reminisce of times they shared with Mr. Billy, Miss Estelle, and their cousin Jill. Where their names appeared on the program, the name was spelled *Faulkner.* They too had fallen under Mr. Billy's spell. Mr. Billy's spelling of the family name was proliferating and spreading vertically in the branches of the family tree and was taking hold on younger generations of Falkners.

Why had Mr. Billy changed the spelling of his name? He was a master at creating little mysteries in his writings, often leaving the reader to ponder many years before learning or guessing the answer to his implantations in the mind. He answered some of the mysteries he had created in *Sanctuary* in 1930, when, about twenty years later, he published *Requiem for a Nun.* It is probable that his greatest masterpiece of mystery may be that concerning the change of his own name. Even his brother Johncy who authored a number of books, including *My Brother Bill, Chooky,* and *Dollar Cotton,* was unable to say with certainty what the origin or purpose of the change of name might have been, although he himself was entrapped into changing his own name to conform. Johncy hinted that the *u* addition to Falkner to make it Faulkner may have been some ancient spelling of the family name to which Mr. Billy brought reversion. Johncy went on to explain that after he had become a writer himself, Mr. Billy helped him to get a start with publishers and used his influence to attain this end. The publisher inquired as to why he, Johncy, used a spelling of the family name which was different from the way his brother spelled his name. The publisher probably thought there would be some value in the marketplace of the *Faulkner* spelling.

James Nunnery, a contemporary, a close friend, and a fellow drinker of moonshine whiskey of Mr. Billy, by his own account in an article entitled "Falkner with a U" published in 1977, attributes the name change to an erroneous spelling of the Falkner name on a check which a publisher sent to Mr. Billy. It was overdue in terms of Mr. Billy's needs. He wrote that instead of returning the check for re-drafting with the correct spelling, Mr. Billy simply endorsed it with the spelling as it was and got his hands on the cash and thereafter used that spelling of his name.

Joseph Blotner, Mr. Billy's biographer, in his book entitled *Faulkner: A Biography* appears to have documented the origin of the *u* in the Faulkner name as early as 1918 when, in order to join the Royal Canadian Air Force, Mr. Billy claimed to have been born in England, with the name spelled Faulkner.

J. M. Faulkner, known as Jimmy, Mr. Billy's nephew, in a program presented at the Faulkner and Yoknapatawpha Conference in 1988 at the University of Mississippi, indicated that a family spelling its name Faulkner migrated to Maryland from England in the early seventeenth century but that no direct connection was established with the Falkners of Oxford and that family of Maryland Faulkners. It thus seems as if the uncertainty concerning the *u* in Faulkner will beget still other theories. They seemed to have been compounded when I learned that, although Mr. Billy used the Faulkner spelling when his name appeared as an author, he kept his name listed in the Oxford telephone directory as "Falkner, William." In the 1960 directory, however, his name was listed as "Faulkner, William." I wondered if such change in 1960 may have been intended as the correction of a perceived error in the omission of the *u* in Mr. Billy's name. I noted, however, that in the 1961 and 1962 directories Mr. Billy's name was again spelled without the *u*, thus reverting to the traditional Falkner spelling of the family name.

Had Mr. Billy directed the 1960 spelling of the Falkner family name, with the *u* inserted? Had Mr. Billy used the telephone directory to align himself with, or to validate, the Faulkner spelling by a growing number of his relatives who had adopted that spelling of their family name?

Did Mr. Billy consider the Faulkner spelling of his name as only a pen name, a nom de plume, to be used in his publications, while preferring to be known as a Falkner by the people of Oxford? Did Mr. Billy intend to change the family's name when he originally began to use the Faulkner name?

Whatever may have been Mr. Billy's intentions remains obscure. To me, however, some results of his insertion of the *u* in the spelling of his family name became very clear. I discovered that twenty-two years after Mr. Billy's death in 1962 his spelling of Falkner with a *u* had been adopted and propagated by his relatives who preferred the Faulkner spelling.

In the 1984 Oxford telephone directory I found that there were eight listings under the Faulkner name, including that of Mr. Billy's nephew, J. M. ("Jimmy") Faulkner, while there were only three listings under the Falkner name, including that of Mr. Billy's other nephew, and Jimmy's brother, M. C. ("Chooky") Falkner.

All of the above speculations and theories concerning the introduction of the *u* into the spelling of the Falkner name by Mr. Billy must be judged in the light of the following quotation from *A History of Mississippi* by Robert Lowry and William S. McCardle, published in New Orleans and New York by University Publishing Company in 1893.

> John M. Stone became Governor of Mississippi on March 19, 1876. He was a native of Gibson County, Tennessee, but had for many years been a citizen of Tishomingo County, Mississippi. He entered the Confederate service as Captain of a company of the Second Regiment of Mississippi Infantry and after the resignation of Colonel W. C. Faulkner became Colonel of that regiment.

The presence of the *u* in the name of Mr. Billy's great-grandfather might change the inquiry regarding the origin of the *u* in the Faulkner name to a question as to when and why the *u* was removed from the spelling used in the name of Mr. Billy's great-grandfather.

I mentioned the 1893 spelling of the Old Colonel's name with the *u* included to Jimmy Faulkner. Jimmy said that sometimes his great-great-grandfather spelled his name both ways, that he had had both spellings on his stationery, and that while the original spelling included the *u*, the Old Colonel dropped the *u* from his name because another family in Tippah County whom he did not like spelled its name with the *u*.

Jimmy said that the Old Colonel had helped build the railroad through that county and there was some consideration given to naming it the Falkner Railroad, but the Old Colonel had said that he would settle for the naming of the railroad station Falkner Station and that this was the origin of the name of Falkner, Mississippi.

Jimmy also told me that he had recently become the grandfather of a grandson who has been named John Wesley Thompson Faulkner V.

My attention was unexpectedly focused upon Mr. Billy's inge-

The Tombstone of Dr. John Taylor
John Taylor was one of the earliest white settlers in the vicinity of Taylor, Mississippi, coming to the territory in about 1811. Some scholars believe that Faulkner derived the Sartoris family name from the Taylor family name by using the Greek word *sartoris,* which means "tailor."

Photo courtesy of Herman E. Taylor

nuity in the creation of the family name *Sartoris,* which appeared in many of his novels.

One morning in August of 1985 during the Faulkner and Yoknapatawpha Conference, Dr. James Hinkle, an English professor from San Diego State University, approached me at the Alumni House on the Ole Miss campus inquiring as to any information I might have on one John Taylor, for whom the town of Taylor was named. Dr. John Taylor, my great-great-grandfather, had been born in North Carolina in 1788, the son of Captain Daniel Taylor of the Continental Army from North Carolina. John Taylor had come from North Carolina to Mississippi around the year 1810. Dr. Hinkle was quite excited when he learned that Dr. John was in the vicinity of what would later become known as Taylor, Mississippi, many years before the Treaty of Pontotoc Creek of 1832. After that treaty, former Indian lands could be bought, and settlers came into the region in increasing numbers. Dr. Hinkle was even more excited when he learned that John Taylor's family was documented in the census of 1850, which described houses by number and listed those who lived there.

In the course of this conversation, Dr. Hinkle asked, "Do you know what *Sartoris* means in Greek?" I confessed that I did not and had never even thought of it. I had wondered at times about such a name being picked by Mr. Billy for the name of the family which would appear in many of his novels including the one entitled *Sartoris.* I had never heard of anyone who lived in Mississippi having such a name and had wondered why Mr. Billy had chosen that particular name. Dr. Hinkle then said, "In Greek, *sartoris* is a word meaning 'tailor'."

A chill ran down my spine as the implications of this took shape in my mind. Why had Mr. Billy picked a name like Sartoris for the name of a family which seemed to resemble the Falkner family in history and characteristics, including the Old Colonel as the railroad builder, the Young Colonel as president of the local bank, and the daredevil tendency toward self-destruction of the younger males of the Sartoris family? Members of the Falkner family could be perceived as having inspired Mr. Billy to create some of the characters appearing in his writings.

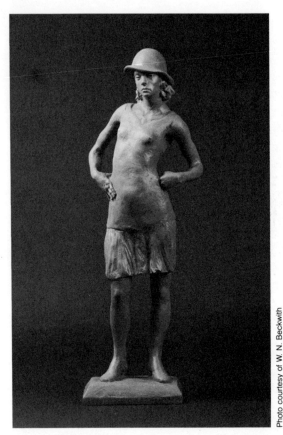

Temple Drake
Sculptor William N. Beckwith of Taylor, Mississippi, made a bronze statue of Temple Drake as he conceived her to have appeared in *Sanctuary*. The statue is twenty-four inches in height. A reproduction of the statue was presented to Ruth Ford for her portrayal of Temple in the Broadway production of *Requiem for a Nun*.

Photo courtesy of W. N. Beckwith

Gradually I began to reflect upon the possibility that Mr. Billy had chosen the family name of one of the earliest settlers in the region, that of John Taylor, as the origin of the mythical family he created and named Sartoris.

After my initial readings of some of Mr. Billy's books, I noted that, with the exception of Taylor, Mississippi, Mr. Billy rarely mentioned any identifiable location in Lafayette County by its actual name. In *Sanctuary*, Taylor was the destination of Gowan Stevens in his drunken drive to intercept the train on which Temple Drake was riding.

To one familiar with Lafayette County, the innuendos abound which indicate that Taylor may have been one locale which stimu-

Photo courtesy of Jack Cofield

Taylor's Depot
The Mississippi Central Railroad was built through Taylor in the late 1850s. In *Sanctuary,* Temple Drake left a special train loaded with Ole Miss students at the Taylor Depot, thus beginning her sensational adventures.

lated his imagination. The Yocona River flows near Taylor. The highest point in the county is Thacker's Mountain, about two or three miles north of Taylor. The railroad crossing where horses were killed by a train in *The Town,* could have been where the railroad crossed the Old Taylor Road, about two miles north of Taylor. The Yocona River bends to the southwest direction near Taylor and could have influenced the choice of Frenchman's Bend as his mythical hamlet. John Taylor had leased land from the Chickasaw Indians before it could be bought. He received patents, signed by President Martin Van Buren, to most of the land near Taylor around 1839. He is said to have built the first water-powered mill in Lafayette County. In addition to practicing medicine and farming, he served as the first postmaster and first station master when the railroad came to Taylor's Depot.

Very little in Mr. Billy's writings appears to depict any of John Taylor's progeny. They became farmers, merchants, ministers, teachers, physicians, lawyers, and soldiers. Three of Dr. John Taylor's grandsons, Benjamin S., Robert G., and Joseph Lane, served in the Confederate Army. Robert was killed and Joseph Lane lost an arm in the Battle of Shiloh. Dr. John died of a heart attack as Yankee occupation troops approached his home on November 5, 1865. He was buried in the Yocona Cemetery near Taylor. The Taylors bore little resemblance to the recklessly adventuresome Sartoris clan.

Mr. Billy had created the purely fictional family name of Sartoris and made its members more like Falkners than Taylors. I further surmised that the use of an actual family name like Taylor would have caused Mr. Billy's characters to be too nearly identifiable and not sufficiently fictional. Mr. Billy may have found it desirable to derive a pseudonym for Taylor, and that "tailor" translated into Latin turned out to be *sartorius,* but by re-translation of the Latin *sartorius* to its Greek equivalent, the word *sartoris* (without the *u*) is found.

If it be assumed that there may have been some connection in Mr. Billy's mind between the names Taylor and Sartoris in creating a fictional name then changing the *y* in Taylor to *i* and transposing "tailor" to the Greek *sartoris,* was an ingenious innovation which can be understood by everyone. Mr. Billy's reason for changing his own name by the addition of the letter *u* may never be truly understood by anyone.

Chapter 8

Roads

Nearly all main roads in Lafayette County lead to Oxford or to other roads which do. Many of Mr. Billy's novels concern events that occurred along these roads. Traveling on these roads would move his imagination as he created the characters, plots, and action of his fiction.

I found myself continually trying to identify the roads on which Mr. Billy's stories had been envisaged. One of the few identifications I felt certain about was found in *Sanctuary*. In that novel it was at Taylor on "the old road to Taylor" that Temple Drake began her travels that would take her to adventures in a bootlegger's home, a rape in a corn crib, a murder, and her stay in a Memphis house of prostitution.

Most of the roads have now been straightened, widened, and improved. Some of them have been abandoned and obscured by erosion and vegetation such as honeysuckle, blackberry vines, plum thickets, and weeds that grow on poor subsoil of sand and clay. Other old roads, once abandoned, have been reconstructed and improved as has "the old road to Taylor." Its name has been changed to the Old Taylor Road.

Geography, history, economics, the spirit of adventure, and a craving for the ownership of land all contributed to the building of the roads for the settlement of Lafayette County, and the creation of Mr. Billy's mythical Yoknapatawpha County in its likeness.

Foot Paths and Wagon Trails

The deer runs and footpaths of the Indian, the hunter, and the explorer became the wagon trails along the ridge tops by which the early settlers came into what would become Lafayette County. They established trading posts and settlements at Oxford, Taylor, Abbeville, Yocona, Tula, and Burgess, and began to dispossess the Chickasaw Indians, to clear the land and propagate their kind, and to populate Lafayette County. The stagecoach, and eventually the railroad and the automobile, would cause a continual evolution in the ways of life in this county.

The road net near Oxford in the early 1900s might be likened to a wagon wheel with roads as spokes leading from the hub, represented by Oxford, outward into all parts of the county. Beyond Lafayette County these "spoke" roads led to Holly Springs to the north, New Albany and Pontotoc to the east, Water Valley to the south, Batesville and Sardis to the west, and Senatobia to the northwest.

Along these roads would move all segments of society including the forces of law and order—the sheriff and the posse, or a lynch mob impatient for swift "justice," the lawyer and the judge intent upon honing the lines of distinction between legality and illegality; the politician promising to please all who might vote for him; the country doctor with pills and potions making house calls in his buggy; the parson and circuit rider defining and damning sin, the righteous and the unrighteous, the pious and the licentious, the poor and the rich, the forces of good and evil moving in tandem or side by side and changing positions as moods, impulses, and rewards might change. Also there were the bootleggers and their runners, as well as the farmer with his wagon heavily laden with cotton, corn, or logs for milling, and freshly killed beef or pork, vegetables or firewood to be peddled from door to door in town. Sometimes there might even be a herd of cattle being driven to the marketplace.

Why had these people come to be in my town and county? What circumstances or conflicts of family, church, law, politics, or economics had brought the early settler to this place of poor hilly land between small and scarcely navigable rivers in the remote reaches of the Atlantic colonies or states?

The quest for adventure or desire to escape their position in their earlier social and economic castes might have drawn the earliest settlers here. On foot, horseback, and by wagon train on trails through the woods the explorers and settlers moved. They would clear the trails across the Piedmont plateau and mountains to the west. They moved through the Cumberland and Newfound gaps and came into the land sloping westwardly. There the rainfall drained into the streams and rivers which for hundreds of miles flowed across the great Mississippi Valley. Here was land and plenty of it. Here at last was opportunity where the settlers might find their destiny, working the land and building their villages, towns, schools, churches, homes, and businesses. In the process they would themselves become the new establishment. Some might become members of the landed aristocracy. Others would follow their adventuresome impulses even farther to the west.

Overland travel into the Mississippi Territory on foot or by wagon train over upland trails had formidable difficulties, particularly for settlers with families. Was there a better way to reach the desired location for settlement?

Rivers to the west formed beneath the towering mountains of the Carolinas, Virginia, and Tennessee. The "over the hills country" would become the states of Tennessee, Kentucky, Alabama, and Mississippi. The Little Tennessee, the French Broad, and many other rivers flowed into the Tennessee River. It ran south, then west across Alabama to northeast Mississippi, then north across both Tennessee and Kentucky to join the Ohio River which then fed into the great Mississippi. The Mississippi River touched the borders of Kentucky, Illinois, Missouri, Arkansas, Tennessee, Mississippi, and Louisiana. This network of rivers became the highways of the pioneers. The river currents could move log rafts and transport these pioneers to the lands along the rivers for a thousand miles or more, passing high bluffs along the way where settlements sprang up which would be known as Knoxville, Chattanooga, Memphis, Vicksburg, and Natchez. Finally New Orleans might be reached and there log rafts could be sold for capital to buy land and begin the better way of life which some sought, or the money could be squandered at the gambling table or in a brothel.

The explorers, then the hunters, then the traders, came into the

Mississippi Territory but soon left without doing great damage to the Indians. The settlers, however, came and stayed. First they made friends with the Indians, then contrived ways and means of dispossessing them of their ancient landholdings in forests and the wild game upon which their livelihood depended.

Eventually the United States government coerced the Indians to sign treaties such as that of Pontotoc Creek in 1832 by which the Chickasaw Indians ceded the lands in the vicinity of Oxford, Mississippi, to the United States. Patents were then granted to settlers conveying title to them of the former Indian lands.

Mr. Billy described the pathetic scene of the Indian matriarch signing over her tribal lands to government agents and departing for the Indian Territory in his novel *Requiem for a Nun,* published in 1951.

After the Treaty of Pontotoc Creek the Indians owned no land. Without military or political power they were defenseless and were forcibly moved to the Oklahoma Indian Territory.

Settlers who chose to push westward into Mississippi along the Indian trails, turned them into wagon roads on snaking ridges between the streams. They crossed streams only when the hills ran out in the desired direction. Then they would mount the next ridge, the next, and the next, to finally reach the intended destination. If no destination was clearly defined, the adventurer might settle for some place more easily reachable or closer by, or where he might find a job or mate or because he might like the looks of the land or because some relative or friend had preceded him and provided some reason for stopping there.

The westerly movement proceeded rapidly in Tennessee, which was once a part of the North Carolina colony, but which was to become a separate state after the Revolutionary War. The southerly movement into Alabama and Mississippi proceeded a little slower but accelerated after the Revolution, the wars with the Indians, the War of 1812, and the removal of the Indians in the 1830s. The Natchez Trace ran from Nashville to Natchez, crossing the Mississippi territory from northeast to the southwest. It provided an overland trade route from Nashville to Natchez and to settlements between them.

These movements fostered the establishment of trading posts, settlements, towns and cities along the way, usually at a junction of water and land transportation. Settlements were often situated on high land to avoid floods, insects, and disease-infested swamps and low land.

Other trade routes branched off to run along high ground to settlements at the bluffs on the Mississippi River near Memphis or about two hundred miles to the south at Vicksburg.

By 1817 much growth in the population had taken place in the Mississippi Territory, and surveys of the land and divisions into grand divisions, counties, townships, and sections had been made. Its political existence as a state was begun when it became a state of the United States in 1817.

Lafayette County was created by the legislature in 1836. Oxford, the county seat, is situated near the center of Lafayette County at an elevation of about 500 feet above sea level, and it lies between the Yacona and Tallahatchie rivers. Being sufficiently distant from the swamps and "bottom lands" of both rivers, Oxford escaped the ravages of the yellow fever epidemics of the late 1800s. The yellow fever epidemic of 1898 all but decimated the populations of Taylor and Orwood. Both communities were near the Yocona River swamps.

The watershed ridge, Woodson Ridge, lies between the Yocona and Tallahatchie river basins, providing a highland route which avoided as much low land as possible in reaching Oxford from the Natchez Trace fifty miles to the northeast. A traveler could cross the county from the east to west without crossing a river by traveling the serpentine trail along the intermittent ridges and hills.

South of Oxford this watershed ridge runs near the old road from Oxford to Taylor. The land rises to its highest point in the county at Thacker's Mountain which is two or three miles to the north of Taylor. The mountain rises to an elevation of 629 feet above sea level. That is not a great height for a "mountain," but it was sufficiently high to cause the Confederate forces that were retreating before the Yankees commanded by Maj. Gen. A. J. Smith in 1864 to build fortifications and artillery emplacements on its slopes to impede the invaders' advance. According to Mr. Billy in

Requiem for a Nun, the Yankees had broken through the Confederate defenses along Hurricane Creek, four miles north of Jefferson near the site of the plantation of John Sartoris.

Country Roads

From the town square of Oxford the streets lead to the city limits, beyond which run the rural roads. I imagined these roads to be going to a rim which, being circular or elliptical, would fit within the square corners of the boundaries of the county. Each spoke would be no longer than a day's walk or ride by wagon, buggy, or on the back of a horse or mule. Such a distance would be in the range of fifteen to twenty miles from Oxford. These distant "corner" hamlets or communities would include Tula in the southeast, Orwood in the southwest, Harmontown in the northwest, and Philadelphia in the northeast corner of the county.

Along such roads would be villages or communities at about a half day's journey, that is, from six to ten miles from the square of Oxford. From these nearby communities one might go by horse to Oxford and return home after tending to business within a single day. These communities were Taylor and Fudgetown to the south, Yocona, Mount Zion, and Woodson Ridge to the east, Abbeville and College Hill to the north, and Burgess to the west. A round trip to Oxford from the more distant villages required a full day's travel, more or less, on horseback or by buggy or might require several hours in a Model-T Ford, allowing time to fix a flat tire or to be pulled out of a mud hole.

Tula, near the southeast corner of the county, is thought by many Faulkner scholars to have been the inspiration for Mr. Billy's mythical Frenchman's Bend. Mr. Billy's map of Yoknapatawpha County in *Absalom, Absalom* placed the Old Frenchman's Place near Tula.

Before the 1920s the road that was wide enough for wagons pulled by mules to pass each other was wide enough for most of the activities which occurred along the rural roads in the county. These roads provided the principal transportation routes within the county, and they usually ran to the nearest village and thence to Oxford.

The roads usually followed along ridges and from hill to hill. Scarcely a hill can be found that does not preserve the evidence of iron rimmed wagon wheels cutting through the topsoil crust, thus allowing ensuing rainfalls to wash the silt away, to clog streams and cover valley bottoms while leaving gullies and depressions where once a road had been. If the road became so bad that wagons and trucks mired up to their axles, it might be "corduroyed." Trees of about six inches in diameter would be cut and trimmed to poles, and these would be laid parallel to each other and across the traffic lane to keep wagon or truck wheels from sinking deep in the bog when heavily loaded. Mr. Billy describes such "corduroying" of roads in *The Reivers.*

With the advent of the truck and automobile in increasing numbers, the need for a greater width of roads necessitated widening and straightening of these roads, the bridging of rivers and creeks, and the building of levees across swamps. It became a political imperative which would require a half-century to accomplish, eventually permitting the movement from place to place with greater speed and safety, and stimulating travel, commerce, and education, accelerating the growth of larger towns at the expense of hamlets and rural communities. For the half century following the horse and buggy era, the promises of political campaigns in Mississippi would center upon better roads, particularly "farm-to-market" roads.

Improvement was slow but the political pressure was great. It had not been unusual for a road to follow the ridge line for a mile or more to avoid the perils of crossing the valleys, streams, and bogs. These roads finally were improved as traffic increased and voters commanded the attention of politicians at local, state, and national levels. The road improvements reflected the public's demand for better farm to market roads and highways to join expressways which would provide the people of the rural communities with more convenient access to the population centers of the nation.

Some old abandoned roads can be rediscovered in and near Oxford. These may have been the routes which were traveled by the characters in Mr. Billy's novels as they carried mail and hauled the farm products to the trading post at Oxford, which would become the county seat of Lafayette County. It would also become the Jefferson in Faulknerian imagination, where Snopeses and Sartorises would vie for economic power.

Roads Eastward

The old abandoned road which once ran southeast out Lake Street, now Johnson Avenue, descended for about a quarter of a mile, dropping about a hundred feet down a steeply sloping ravine. There it crossed Birney's Branch, and ascended the ridge to the east of Oxford, and ran toward the communities of Yellow Leaf, Fudgetown, Yocona, Tula and the region of Mr. Billy's fictional Frenchman's Bend. This old road appears to have been abandoned in the late 1800s. It had been the main road to the southeast for a long time, and the hills to the east have deep cuts along the route. This old road was abandoned after "old" Highway 6 was built along the top of the ridge to the east of Oxford which allowed traffic from that direction to enter Oxford by East University Avenue.

Since the 1950s the main road to the east from Oxford has been "new" Highway 6 which goes to Pontotoc. When this highway reaches River's Hill, a mile to the east of South Lamar Boulevard, a fork to the south becomes Highway 334 (formerly "old" Highway 6).

Highway 334 connects Oxford with the Yocona community to the southeast in Lafayette County, then runs to Toccopola and Pontotoc in Pontotoc County. It lies a few miles to the south of the "new" Highway 6 between Oxford and Pontotoc.

Highway 334 follows the route which Flem Snopes and his wife, Eula Varner Snopes, in Mr. Billy's novel *The Town*, traveled into Jefferson in a wagon hauling their household goods and the tent in which they would live for several years until Flem became more affluent in his rise to the presidency of the bank.

116

Another spoke in the wheel representing the road net, past and present, is the partly-abandoned road leading to the east of Oxford from Jackson Avenue, formerly called Pontotoc Street or "the hilly street" by older Oxonians. Sometimes this abandoned road was called the Lafayette Springs Road. It paralleled the Falkner Highway, and ran a mile or so to the south of that highway. It crosses the sand-filled and usually dry bed of Birney's Branch, which at this point is not a flowing stream except after heavy rains. The old roadbed runs up and over the ridge to the east of Oxford and crosses the Campground Road, Four Mile Branch, and the hills between it and Yellow Leaf Creek, which is about six miles from Oxford. Yellow Leaf Creek, it seemed to me, is probably the stream which inspired Mr. Billy in *The Hamlet* to call a stream White Leaf Creek. It is a rapidly flowing spring-fed stream beginning near Woodson Ridge and flowing into the Yocona River about five miles to the south.

The Lafayette Springs Road was once the main road from Oxford to Lafayette Springs in Pontotoc County. The road enabled travelers to avoid crossing the Tallahatchie River in coming to Oxford.

In growing up, I had frequently visited my grandparents, James Webster Stephens and Jennie (Mary Jane McLarty) Stephens, who had lived near that road. My grandmother told me that during the late nineteenth century it was a road heavily traveled by wagons, buggies, and riders on horseback.

I learned some interesting history from my great-aunt Matt (Mattie Stephens) Ragland. She told me of Yankee troops who, during the Civil War, came foraging and confiscated all of the livestock. My grandfather, James Webster Stephens, then only seven years old, was told to take the family mare deep into the woods and hide there until the Yankees departed. One of the soldiers knew how to call a horse. When he called, the mare neighed, and the soldiers were able to capture the horse. They also took all of the hogs and chickens, leaving only an old rooster as the sole living animal on the farm.

My Aunt Matt had lived in a log house beside the old road to Lafayette Springs, which had been built by my great-great-grandfather, John David Stephens (1781-1871) and my great-grand-

117

Photo courtesy of Herman E. Taylor

The Stephens-Ragland House
Located on Lafayette Springs Road east of Oxford, this home was the site of the
film production of "Barn Burning." Built about 1858, the house was made from
hand-hewn logs and split wood shingles. It is one of the few remaining log homes
in Lafayette County.

father, John Caanan Stephens (1808-1881). This Stephens-Ragland
log house still stands and was owned, in 1988, by my cousin, Elisabeth Stephens Rounsaville. The house was made of oak timbers
which had been hand hewn from virgin oaks and cut square to
about twelve inches on each of all four sides. The timbers were
about twenty feet in length and were notched at the ends. The
spaces between the timbers were chinked with clay.

There were two such buildings made of hand-hewn timbers
connected by a dog trot, or breezeway, which was about ten feet
wide and provided space for several rocking chairs. In each of
these log rooms there was a fireplace large enough to burn wood
of approximately four feet in length. The fireplaces and chimneys
were made of sandstone, the only rock to be found in the nearby
hills, which was also used as pillars for supporting the buildings.

To the rear of the log rooms were several rooms made of ordi-

118

nary sawn timbers and boards. They appeared to have been added to the log house front rooms to provide space for an additional bedroom, a dining room, and a kitchen.

Drinking water had to be brought from a spring situated across the road and about one hundred yards from the house. An alternate source of drinking water was at a more distant point about two hundred yards away near the foot of The Big Hill to the east of the house. From a spring which was uphill about twenty feet from the foot path, water flowed through a V-shaped wooden trough made by nailing two boards together. Buckets could be filled from this water spout.

There was a split rail fence which encircled the dwelling house, the smokehouse, the chicken house, the privy, and a storage house. To the rear and east of the fence around the dwelling house and outbuildings lay the barnyard in which were situated the barn, the corncrib, and the stables and beyond this was the calf pasture. They, too, were encircled by a split rail fence for a half-mile or more.

The Big Hill was a source of much interest to me, my brother, sister, and a half-dozen cousins, for upon its slopes grew sweet gum, chestnut, and hickory trees, grapes and plums. At the highest point of this hill, at an elevation of about 500 feet above sea level, one could see forever it seemed, but specifically I could see the spire of the Episcopal church and the water tank in Oxford, about eight miles to the west.

It was in this log house that my mother, Kate Stephens (Taylor), had been born on September 27, 1890. On frequent visits to this farm during my youth, I had explored for a couple of miles in all directions for swimming holes, watermelon patches, and sorghum fields, and had hunted squirrels, rabbits, and quail.

This house site and its surroundings was where Mr. Billy's story "Barn Burning" was filmed in 1978 for national public television. In the movie Mr. Billy's nephew, Jimmy Faulkner, played a leading role.

The traffic in the general east-northeast direction from Oxford now uses Mississippi Highway 30, the former route of the Falkner Highway. The old Lafayette Springs Road, for about six miles east

Photo courtesy of Herman E. Taylor

The Old Campground

Since the late 1860s, the campground has been the site of annual Methodist revival meetings. The Tabernacle shelters three or four religious services daily. Maud Falkner attended services here, and William Faulkner often led the Oxford Boy Scout Troop here on overnight hikes.

of Oxford almost to Yellow Leaf Creek, has been abandoned since the early 1900s. The old road, now eroded into the red clay subsoil, can be seen where it crosses the Campground Road about three miles east of Oxford and a mile or so north of the Old Methodist Campground. The Campground Road runs north from Highway 6 to Highway 30. Since 1870 the Old Campground has been the scene of Methodist revival meetings which lasted a week beginning on the first Sunday in August of each year. Mr. Billy, as scout master in Oxford, once led his troop on an overnight hike to this campground and camped in the Tabernacle there. His mother, Miss Maud, sometimes attended these camp meetings according to Mr. Billy's biographer, Joseph Blotner. The Falkners for many years were tent holders at the Campground. I recalled that the Falkner tent adjoined the Temple tent which was owned by E. E. Temple.

Photo courtesy of Herman E. Taylor

The Falkner "Tent" at the Old Campground
The tent included a women's room and a men's room separated by a hallway. At the rear was a dining table and a kitchen area. When the Falkners were no longer active in campground activities, the tent passed into the hands of Guy McLarty and later George Canton.

One of Mr. Billy's most famous characters was Temple Drake in *Sanctuary* and *Requiem for a Nun.*

The route of the old Lafayette Springs Road is discernable to the east and west of the Campground Road. As it progresses through the hills it passes just to the south of Mount Zion Methodist Church, a mile or so to the east.

Mr. Billy, in writing *Requiem for a Nun,* may have had the old road to Lafayette Springs in mind as he described the U.S. mail carrier who rode a pony from Jefferson to Nashville in the period around the 1820s. Mr. Billy fictionalized that the town of Jefferson took its name from the name of the mail carrier. By going along the route of the old Lafayette Springs Road, that mail carrier could have avoided crossing the Tallahatchie River in Lafayette County.

Mississippi Highway 30 lies a few miles to the north of the old

Lafayette Springs Road and leads to the communities of Philadelphia and Etta and thence to New Albany in Union County.

Roads Northward

North of Oxford, Highway 7 runs to Holly Springs. In the 1920s
and 1930s this was the main road from Oxford to Memphis. In Mr.
Billy's novel *The Mansion,* it was along that road that Mink Snopes
traveled to Jefferson for the purpose of killing his cousin Flem
Snopes after he was released from the penitentiary at Parchman.
He left the highway a few miles north of Jefferson, then walked
along the railroad into town.

About a mile or so north of the square on Highway 7 and 30, the
roads separate and Highway 30 proceeds eastward to New Albany,
about thirty miles distant in Union County. Highway 7 continues
northward to Holly Springs, which is also about thirty miles from
Oxford, in Marshall County.

This road juncture was known as Three Way and there was a
service station and grocery store on the east side of the fork. This
was known to be a place where bootleg whiskey could be bought
in the 1920s and 1930s. Once a murder was committed at this
store when one bootlegger shot and killed another one. The
murder described in Mr. Billy's short story included in *Knight's
Gambit* apparently was inspired by the actual murder which had
occurred there.

By the 1980s Three Way had become a four-way intersection. A
new highway called Molly Barr Road led from the area north of the
University of Mississippi in a circling route to this intersection.
Molly Barr Road was named for a Negro woman who had owned
some of the property through which the new road passed. This
road enabled traffic to avoid the city of Oxford with its traffic con-
gestion in going to and from the campus and Highway 6 West to a
new Highway 7 Bypass which was constructed from Oxford to
Holly Springs. This new Highway 7 lay along a route which was
east of the older Highway 7, which was very hilly and crooked.
Highway 7 Bypass, built in the 1970s, ran to the south along

Birney's Branch Bottom and joined Old Highway 7 several miles south of Oxford.

About four miles north of Oxford on Highway 7 was the fictional plantation of John Sartoris, as shown by Mr. Billy's map included in *Absalom, Absalom.*

About ten miles along Highway 7, a traveler would arrive at Abbeville. Continuing on Highway 7, he would find that the highway runs on top of a levee for about two miles. It parallels the railroad tracks which also were situated on top of another levee. The bridges of the railroad and the highway across the Tallahatchie river are much longer than the width of the river channel. This allows the water of the Sardis Reservoir to ebb and flow through the opening in the levees beneath the bridges as the water level of the reservoir rises following heavy rainfalls.

The road is straight and level across the low flat land. North of the bridges and east of the road runs a briskly flowing creek. It flows out of the Wall Doxey State Park a few miles to the north near the town of Waterford.

Downstream along the Tallahatchie River several miles to the west was the area depicted by Mr. Billy in *The Bear.* In it he describes the thick forest or the "big woods" which once covered the land. It was cleared to permit open space for waters of the Sardis Reservoir.

Upstream to the east from the river crossing on Highway 7 was the fictional McCaslin's farm which was a centerpiece of Mr. Billy's novel *Go Down Moses.*

A few miles north of the Tallahatchie River was Malone Tank, one of those watering points where a water supply was available from the creek and could be pumped into a huge tank near the railroad tracks. Steam driven engines would stop there to take on water.

About a mile along Highway 7 northwest of Malone Tank was a country store well known as "the bootlegger's place." Generations of Ole Miss students and Oxonians as well as people from greater distances journeyed there to obtain their illegal but taxable bottles of "black market bonded liquor." There was nothing covert about the operation and usually there was an ample supply.

Lafayette County was "bone dry" on the record of legality in the sale of whiskey, but its people consumed a liberal portion of the liquor sold at this country store. The bootlegger operated just across the Marshall County line.

The owner of that store must have had some sort of understanding with each succeeding sheriff of Marshall County, for a sheriff could serve only four years and could not be reelected without a four-year wait. The store was operated openly with little or no interference from federal, state, or local officials. The sale of alcoholic beverages did not violate federal law.

One analyst explained that Mississippi had the ideal arrangement for the unlawful sale of liquor: People who wanted an alcoholic drink could buy it at the bootlegger's place. The liquor industry and the bootlegger made money without competition, and the churchgoers and others who advocated prohibition could claim that they had a "dry state" for the record. Meanwhile, the state collected a "Black Market Tax." This accommodation continued for several decades in Mississippi, well into the 1960s. A close friend of mine who was a lawyer and later an associate justice of the Mississippi Supreme Court explained to me how the "Black Market Tax" was finally ended.

In 1965, the sheriff serving Hinds County became ill. The circuit judge, a strict Presbyterian layman who hated alcohol in any form, relieved the sheriff and appointed an experienced law enforcement man as acting sheriff. On the night of February 4, 1966, the annual Carnival Ball was held at the Jackson Country Club. This event was the biggest social event for prominent people that was held in Jackson. Governor Paul B. Johnson, Jr., was present as well as many other important officials.

Late in the evening, when the ball was going full blast, the sheriff and his deputies showed up with a search warrant for alcoholic beverages. The sheriff knew the location of the door on the main floor that led to the stored alcohol which was served at the bar. The club officials refused to open the door, so it was broken down with axes, and the bottles containing alcohol were removed while the governor and other officials and influential people looked on.

As soon as the legislature met, its members began laying plans to repeal the prohibition laws of Mississippi. That was accomplished at the legislative session of that year.

Most everyone concedes, I was told, that the "country club affair" was instrumental in repealing the "Black Market Tax" and in legalizing the sale of whiskey in Mississippi, putting the bootleggers out of business.

A new door was installed at the Jackson Country Club storage room, and on it in gold letters was written "Axe and You Shall Receive." It is still there.

Beer

Beer drinkers also had problems with the laws of a dry state or county or town. Local option law allowed towns and counties to prohibit the sale of beer.

From the early 1930s until near the end of World War II, Oxford had allowed the lawful sale of beer in restaurants. During World War II, some say while the majority of beer drinkers were off fighting the war against Hitler and the Japs, an election was held and the voters of Oxford voted to rid the city of lawful beer sales.

In 1950 Mr. Billy championed legalizing the sale of beer in Oxford. When the local newspaper editor refused to publish his views, he employed a printing press and published circulars in which he pointed out the unfairness of holding a "beer election" while the beer drinkers were away in military service.

The Presbyterian, Methodist, and Baptist ministers had published an article in *The Oxford Eagle* in which they had condemned the legal sale of beer. The following is Mr. Billy's reply:

TO THE VOTERS OF OXFORD

EDITOR'S NOTE: This is a re-print of a handbill that William Faulkner had printed at his own expense and personally distributed in Oxford. It is in reply to a statement carried in *The Oxford Eagle* in the 1950s.

Correction to paid printed statement of Private Citizens H. E. Finger, Jr., John K. Johnson, and Frank Moody Purser.

1. "Beer was voted out in 1944 because of its obnoxiousness."

Beer was voted out in 1944 because too many voters who drank beer or didn't object to other people drinking it, were absent in Europe and Asia defending Oxford where voters who preferred home to war would vote on beer in 1944.

2. "A bottle of 4 per cent beer contains twice as much alcohol as a jigger of whiskey."

A 12 ounce bottle of four per cent beer contains forty-eight one hundredths of one ounce of alcohol. A jigger holds one and one-half ounces (see Dictionary). Whiskey ranges from 30 to 45 per cent alcohol. A jigger of 30 per cent whiskey contains forty-five one hundredths of one ounce of alcohol. A bottle of 4 per cent beer doesn't contain twice as much alcohol as a jigger of whiskey. Unless the whiskey is less than 32 per cent alcohol, the bottle of beer doesn't even contain as much.

3. "Money spent for beer should be spent for food, clothing and other essential consumer goods."

By this precedent, we will have to hold another election to vote on whether or not the florists, the picture shows, the radio shops and the pleasure car dealers will be permitted in Oxford.

4. "Starkville and Water Valley voted beer out, why not Oxford?"

Since Starkville is the home of Mississippi State, and Mississippi State beat the University of Mississippi at football, maybe Oxford, which is the home of the University of Mississippi, is right in taking Starkville for a model. But why must we imitate Water Valley? Our high school team beat theirs, didn't it?

Yours for a freer Oxford, where publicans can be law abiding publicans six days a week, and Ministers of God can be Ministers of God all seven days in a week, as the Founder of their Ministry commanded them to when He ordered them to keep out of temporal politics in His own

words: 'Render unto Caesar the things that are Caesar's and
to God the things that are God's.'

William Faulkner
Private Citizen

Mr. Billy's circular was reprinted in the Faulkner Edition of *The
Oxford Eagle* in 1976 and is reprinted with the permission of *The
Oxford Eagle.*

Nevertheless, the "drys" won the election and for nearly thirty
years beer could not be sold legally in Oxford.

Roads Westward

Until the late 1930s there were three dirt or graveled main roads
leading westward from Oxford. The road leading to Burgess and
Batesville ran out University Avenue and through the campus of
the University of Mississippi and south near the university post
office around the power plant, then along what later became Fraternity Row. The other roads went, respectively, to Sardis by way
of Hays Crossing at the Tallahatchie River in Panola County, to
College Hill and northwest towards Senatobia and Memphis. In the
1920s the latter two roads proceeded out College Hill Street, then
divided to go their separate ways.

In the late 1930s Jackson Avenue was extended westward, running beneath the tracks of the Illinois Central Railroad, then
through the woodlands belonging to the university. Near the
northwest corner of the university property a new road, Mississippi Highway 6, was constructed and paved around the west
side of the university. It ran southwest until it joined the Oxford to
Batesville road running through the campus. From there the new
Highway 6, paved with concrete, was built to Batesville, being
completed around 1937.

The road which ran due west from Jackson Avenue ran in a
nearly straight line along the route of the present Highway 314
toward Hays Crossing and Sardis. In the western part of Yoknapatawpha County near Highway 314, Mr. Billy placed the fic-

127

tional plantation of Thomas Sutpen called Sutpen's Hundred. Highway 314 led to Hays Crossing of the Tallahatchie River before the Sardis Reservoir was filled with water in the late 1930s, according to Mr. Billy's map of Yoknapatawpha County in *Absalom, Absalom.*

About a mile and a half west of the Oxford square, just west of the Oxford-University Airport, a road leaves Highway 314 and runs to College Hill. This road was called Lamar Highway on the 1916 map of Lafayette County, but is now called College Hill Road. This road and the Highway 314 route were terminated at the shoreline of Sardis Lake around 1939 when "the world's largest earthen dam," the Sardis Dam, was completed. After that time, traffic to the west of Oxford moved along Highway 6.

By the 1970s Highway 6 was made into a four-lane divided highway around the south side of Oxford and the university, then to Batesville.

Prior to the building of Highway 6 in the 1930s, the route to College Hill had proceeded northwest from College Hill Street, passing the home of Phil Stone, a lawyer and friend of Mr. Billy. I speculated that this was the road which in Mr. Billy's imagination the boys in *The Reivers* traveled in 1905 in their escapade to Memphis which took them to the crossing of the Tallahatchie River near Wyatt, then on through the Hell Creek bottomland. It was there that they encountered the farmer who entrapped them in a muddy bog of his own making and had his mules extricate them from the mud for the price of six dollars, figured at two dollars per passenger.

The land near Mr. Billy's imaginary hunting camp, featured in his story of "The Bear," and the region of Sutpen's Hundred plantation described in *Absalom, Absalom,* and the land near Wyatt's Crossing described in *The Reivers,* was covered by the waters of Sardis Lake.

The northwest parts of Lafayette County were almost isolated from the rest of the county by the Sardis Reservoir. A route by which these parts of Lafayette County may be reached is Highway 310 which runs west near the north side of Sardis Lake from Highway 7 in the vicinity of Malone Tank and proceeds to Como about twenty-five miles to the west.

There was no public transportation from Oxford to the west until the mid-1930s. The railroad ran from Oxford to the north and south. There has never been a direct railroad service between the hills where Oxford is located and the Delta to the west and north of the Columbus, Greenwood, and Greenville line. In order to get to Oxford, anyone in the Delta had to go by train to Memphis aboard the "Y. and M.V." (the Yazoo and Mississippi Valley) line, sometimes called "The Yellow Dog," or the branch of the Illinois Central which ran north near the Mississippi River from New Orleans, to Natchez, to Vicksburg, Greenville, and Clarksdale. From Memphis, the traveler had to ride the Frisco railroad to Holly Springs, then change to another branch of the Illinois Central for the ride to Oxford.

If one had chosen to go by automobile there would be many miles on dirt or graveled roads over and through the hills to finally reach Oxford and the University of Mississippi. Reaching the university, for most travelers, may have been the principal reason for making the trip.

It was the Wasson Bus Line of Clarksdale which first connected the Delta and the hills by public transportation along such roads as existed in the middle 1930s.

Roads Southward

To the south of Oxford there are now two paved roads, Highway 7 (formerly called the Jefferson Davis Highway) and the Old Taylor Road. Highway 7 was the principal route for traffic during most of Mr. Billy's lifetime. It leads due south from the town square and proceeds out South Lamar Boulevard. It passes the original Oxford Airport where Mr. Billy took flying lessons, and the former location of the county farm called the Poor House, which may have inspired mention of the Poor House in Mr. Billy's novel *Sartoris.* Highway 7 then continues about four miles to Markette's farm along the Yocona River. This road crosses the river at that point, and south of the river, the road forks east and west. In the late 1930s, the "new" Oxford airport was built near the west. The west road runs down the valley a few miles and turns south to the city of Water Valley, about nineteen miles from Oxford along that route. The east fork, now Mississippi Highway 9W, leads to Pittsboro and Bruce. From Water Valley, Highway 7 runs on south to Coffeeville and Grenada.

The second road to the south of Oxford is the Old Taylor Road, which leaves the southwest corner of the corporate limits of Oxford and leads to the town of Taylor about eight miles from Oxford, then goes on to Water Valley.

About a quarter of a mile to the west of South Lamar the Old Taylor Road turns southward. On the northwest side of that turn is situated Mr. Billy's home, which he named Rowan Oak.

The Old Taylor Road was a very old road which once had been the stage coach route and later the railroad paralleled the road. It became a favorite hiking and horseback riding road of Mr. Billy's. Very little traffic used the road in the 1940s and early 1950s.

Most traffic from the vicinity of Taylor bound for Oxford went east from Taylor on a graveled road (presently Mississippi 328) through the foothills north of the Yocona River to state Highway 7. That highway is about five miles east of Taylor in the vicinity of Markette's farm. Thus the "old road to Taylor" fell into disuse and disrepair. Sometimes the bridges were not repaired or replaced for long periods of time, preventing use of that road going to or from Oxford. However, later in the 1950s that road gained in usage after the Chambers range factory was built near it. New houses were built along the higher elevations on the ridge leading towards Thacker's Mountain. The factory was situated between the "old road to Taylor" and the railroad. This old road was re-opened, paved with black top, straightened, and improved all of the way to Taylor.

The name Old Taylor Road was made the official name of the "old road to Taylor."

Within Oxford there are two branches of Old Taylor Road. A second branch of the Old Taylor Road was constructed in the 1960s. This branch runs from the east end of the University Bridge over the railroad south along what was once called Mill Street. It connects with the older branch by way of Taylor Drive north of the Highway 6 Bypass.

To accurately describe which Old Taylor Road one may be speaking of, it becomes necessary to describe this newer road as the "new" Old Taylor Road. The official name of the "new" old Taylor Road is Taylor Road.

Along the west side of the "old" Old Taylor Road are the ten acres of Bailey's Woods which stand along the east boundary of the university property and border the south side of Mr. Billy's home.

The rationale for naming these roads so as to include the Taylor name in each may have been to establish more directly the connection between the road on which is situated Rowan Oak with the main campus of the university which lies to the west about a half-mile. Rowan Oak on the "old" Old Taylor Road is now owned by the university, and it adjoins the university property. By following the Old Taylor roads, new and old, until they are joined by Taylor Drive, visitors and tourists may be guided more easily from the main Ole Miss campus west of the railroad to Rowan Oak where the great novelist lived and wrote for three decades.

South of the four-lane divided highway the Old Taylor Road is a two-lane highway for several miles to the little town of Taylor which Mr. Billy frequently visited. This road provides a panoramic view for many miles as it ascends the elevation near Thacker's Mountain and descends into the valley of Taylor Creek.

County Roads

Some of the roads in the county in the 1920s and 1930s had been but slightly improved since the early settlement of Lafayette County. The county road system remained far behind the state and federal highway system for many years. Part of this problem was attributable to the governmental system having jurisdiction over the local county roads.

A supervisor was elected by the voters in each civil district of the county which was called a beat. The Board of Supervisors constituted the governing body for the county. That body levied taxes and had great autonomy in the building and maintenance of the county roads. Politics reached a fevered heat at this most basic level of government. It was not unusual for violence to erupt at polling places within the rural beats on election day and on some occasions shots might be exchanged between the clan-like supporters of the candidates.

The autonomy of the supervisor included the right to employ workers and to procure equipment and supplies. If a person supported the winning candidate, he could count on having his driveway graveled upon request and members of his family hired to work on the roads. Sometimes the supervisor diverted funds to his own personal use instead of to the building and maintenance of the roads. Kickbacks from equipment suppliers and contractors were not unusual. This tended to reduce the funds actually used for road improvement. Nevertheless, the practice continued for many years.

In the 1980s, however, the federal government entered the picture, and many supervisors across the state found themselves indicted and convicted. This coincided with the massive expenditures incident to the paving and improvement of the farm-to-market roads which politicians had promised for more than half a century.

As technological progress brought the automobile, the demand increased for better roads. Better roads made the labor force more mobile. Alternative jobs became more accessible and less labor was utilized in the growing, harvesting, ginning, and shipment of cotton. No longer did the mere ownership of land license economic exploitation and tyranny as depicted by Mr. Billy in *The Hamlet* when Jody Varner agreed to "furnish" the sharecropper Snopes for one-fourth of the cotton and one-third of the corn and to be repaid for the "furnish" with "six bit dollars."

The period of the Great Depression in the 1930s in Lafayette County may have inspired Mr. Billy to write of the changing conditions and the emerging of the poor, both white and black, into a better economic and social condition, one scarcely imaginable in earlier periods when the landless had to accept the landlord's terms or move out of the community, as described in the "Barn Burning" episode of *The Hamlet*.

The provincial society of Mr. Billy's Yoknapatawpha County was destined to become more mobile and thus more independent of barriers to advancement designed to preserve the status quo for the establishment. The remaining relics of something resembling a feudal system in agriculture, business, and politics were disappearing. Better roads and greater mobility extended economic, social, and political interests beyond the nearest hamlet and town.

The Changing Rural Scene

When a single Lafayette County School was established near Oxford, the local school districts with their one-room schools and even the larger schools at Burgess, Yocona, Taylor, and Abbeville ceased to exist. Children of the most remote areas of the county began attending the Lafayette County School. There the advantages of size included better teachers and physical facilities. Educational opportunities were equalized, homogenized, and standardized for black and white, rich and poor of the county.

The little privately-owned hospitals gave way to the larger county hospital with a greater capacity for medical care and with specialization beyond that previously provided by the general practitioner. The county roads made such centralized facilities accessible to all who lived within the county.

Along the roads of the county, the crews of the Rural Electrification Association brought power to rural homes. This eliminated many of the traditional hardships of rural living.

Increasingly, the rural population shifted from dependency upon agricultural production to employment in Oxford or in distant towns or industries, returning to the farm as such employment permitted. Many held on to their land, unwilling to become members of the landless class, preferring instead to become absentee landlords.

The crossroads country stores, like that of Will Varner in Frenchman's Bend in Mr. Billy's novels *The Hamlet* and *The Town,*

133

began to disappear as great merchandising chains brought the goods of the world to within a short drive of all who once had been the captive customers of the little stores. The massive changes in the roads and in the way of life in Lafayette County occurred within the forty years, more or less, during which Mr. Billy wrote.

Highway Building

Road building in Mississippi became a major industry in the 1930s. Mississippi had long been known as a state for tourists to avoid because of the poor roads it provided. Despite the economic depression, or possibly because of it and the jobs such a program might provide, a massive road building program got under way. A Highway Commission was established and F. L. ("Abe") Linker of Oxford sought election to the post of highway commissioner for North Mississippi. A band of high school musicians, of which I was a member, under the direction of R. Roy Coates, and others who would participate, toured the northern part of the state from Columbus to Corinth to the east, and from Greenwood to Hernando to the west drumming up votes for Abe. A colorful and entertaining merchant of Oxford named Ira L. ("Shine") Morgan served as master of ceremonies in the little towns where the cavalcade stopped. He told several jokes, including the one about a little minnow which had had a drink of moonshine liquor before being put on a hook by a fisherman. Shortly thereafter, according to Shine, "that little bitty minnow was choking the hell out of a great big catfish." It never failed to gain a round of applause. Abe was elected.

Roads in Mississippi had traditionally passed through the centers of towns, making it impossible to travel far without slowing for local traffic in and around the towns with courthouse squares and snarled traffic patterns. Abe designed a highway system which skirted the towns and ignored the desires of local political powers who wanted the highways to come by their property and through their business district.

Highway 61, which ran south from Memphis and down the Mississippi Delta to Leland, then on to Vicksburg and New Orleans, provided a test for this new concept of highway construction. Stretches of many miles of straight, level, two-lane highway were built. The temptation to speed and race or doze at the wheel cost many lives as collisions multiplied. "Death Here" signs were placed so frequently along the road that they sometimes re-sembled a picket fence. Some people thought that the signs did more harm than good and finally they were removed. The mere removal of the signs, however, did not diminish the slaughter in-duced by the temptation to drive at high speeds along these straightaways.

During this road-building decade, nearly everyone who had any skill or experience as a highway engineer found employment in the building of the highways. Among such engineers was Johncy Falkner, Mr. Billy's brother. Often Johncy wore cavalry boots which extended up nearly to his knees, and usually they were cov-ered with mud when he appeared in Oxford. The road crews, in-cluding engineers, sometimes lived in camps along the routes which they were surveying, or where they were supervising con-struction. One story which I heard was to the effect that while the construction crews were near Tunica, Mississippi, building High-way 61, Mr. Billy came to visit Johncy and walked up to the camp appearing to have waded in mud above his knees. He had an ample supply of whiskey with which to celebrate their reunion.

A little later on, about 1936, construction of Mississippi High-way 6, which crossed the state from east to west, from Tupelo to Oxford, Batesville, Marks, and Clarksdale, got under way. It was completed from Oxford to Batesville within two or three years, and the highway from Batesville to Clarksdale was completed by 1941, and for the first time it became possible for me to drive from Oxford to Clarksdale upon a concrete-surfaced highway.

With the completion of the highways to the east, west, north, and south, Mississippi began to become a closer knit community. One could go from the north end of the state to the Gulf Coast in about eight hours, or cross the state from east to west in about three hours.

Before completion of Mississippi Highway 6, there had been

135

very little social mixing, communication, or commerce to the west between the people of Oxford in the hills and people in the Delta. In the late 1930s when the highway was completed all of that began to change. Thereafter, traffic picked up and the people who lived along the highway, whether in the hills or Delta, began to become acquainted. Farm products could be hauled across the state for processing. No longer was it necessary for most commerce in and out of North Mississippi to pass through Memphis, Tennessee. The "hard road," as it was called, referred to Highway 51, which had been paved to Memphis and south to Jackson by the mid-1930s. The juncture of Mississippi Highway 6 and U.S. Highway 51 at Batesville became a favorite meeting place and melting pot and traffic hub for much of North Mississippi. Ole Miss students for generations thereafter would flock to honky-tonks on Highway 51 where beer was legally sold and served and where dance bands played on Saturday nights. Distinctions between rural and urban lifestyles were beginning to disappear as the highways made travel easier.

Passing Trains

When Mr. Billy wrote his earlier stories, it was not easy to travel from Oxford to any distant place except by rail. Many of his novels contain vivid descriptions of the roads along which the people moved in buggies and wagons, then in cars, before the roads were widened, straightened, bridged, paved, and made more usable. He wrote of the post-World War I period as the horse and buggy was being outmoded and replaced by automobiles. The change from horse-drawn carriages to the automobile was noted by Mr. Billy in *Sartoris* in 1929. He told of the changes he foresaw as the horses were retired to idle their lives away as they were replaced by automobiles.

The railroad's business had begun to wane as roads improved, and most people acquired automobiles and traveled when possible by motor vehicle on the roads. There was no longer much demand for passenger service by the trains.

In the mid-1930s, the Tri-State Bus Company began service from

Memphis to Oxford. At first the buses ran by way of Holly Springs to Oxford, then on to Tupelo, fifty miles east of Oxford. Later on when Highway 6 was completed, buses ran to Oxford by way of Batesville. At Batesville, connections could be made to go to the north or south. Bus service proved popular and took from the railroad most of its remaining passenger haul.

Better roads also took much of the freight business away from the railroads. Trucks of ever increasing size could haul freight from the loading dock of the shipper to that of the buyer, thereby eliminating handling costs. The great savings in labor costs sealed the fate of the railroad.

Mr. Billy had traveled extensively and his early travels were mainly by train. In his 1925 novel *Soldier's Pay,* he described train travel in detail. Travel by rail continued to be a feature of his novels written from the 1920s to the 1950s, and he continued describing travel by train in *The Town* written in 1956.

Why Oxford?

In his writings, Mr. Billy could transform Lafayette County into his own domain of imagination and call it Yoknapatawpha County, wherein most every person known to him played some part. Every person who traveled the roads of Lafayette County might become part of a drama to unfold and a story to be told.

Mr. Billy himself explained his selection of Oxford and Lafayette County as the subject matter for his writings. He said that it would take him a lifetime to learn as much about some other place and in such case he would have no time to write of what he learned. He wrote this to Malcolm Cowley, according to the latter's introduction to *The Portable Faulkner.*

Oxford was Mr. Billy's home, and his mother, father, and brothers lived there. It would always be the place to which he would return and where he would spend most of his life. I considered all of this but remained unsatisfied that this was all there was to the reasons for Mr. Billy's returning to Oxford to do most of his writing. Was there some other and more profound and compelling force which brought Mr. Billy back to Oxford and Lafayette County where his roots would renew their growth?

It occurred to me that in the 1920s, Mr. Billy probably would have realized that it would be to Oxford that sooner or later his true love of teenage years might return, even if for no more than a visit with her parents, and where he might see her once again. Whether my speculation was correct or not as to Mr. Billy's motives in returning to Oxford to live and write, such imagined events did in fact occur. In 1924 Miss Estelle had scarcely had time to unpack her luggage upon her return to the Oldham's home from Shanghai and her unsuccessful marriage, accompanied by her two children and a Japanese maid, before Mr. Billy came calling. By 1929 her divorce from Cornell Franklin was finalized. In a borrowed car and with borrowed money, Mr. Billy and Miss Estelle drove out the road to College Hill and found a minister who would pronounce them man and wife on June 20, 1929.

Chapter 9

Rambling

What great writing has there ever been
Without inspiration to begin?

W hat inspiration, aspiration, or motivation enabled a high
school and college "drop-out" to win the Nobel Prize for literature? Intrigued by the incongruity of that occurrence, I sought
answers by reviewing some of the instances when Mr. Billy
Faulkner and I shared the environment of Oxford and that of the
University of Mississippi. Could Mr. Billy's creative genius have
been inspired, aroused, or driven by that environment?

   In the early 1980s I went back home to Oxford and Ole Miss to
refresh my recollections. I stayed in the Alumni House on campus,
which is situated on the site of Mr. Billy's home from 1918 to 1929.

Perspectives

I strolled to the University Bridge which was over The Cut
through the narrowest part of the ridge on which the campus and
much of Oxford was situated. It runs above the tracks of the Illinois Central Railroad, and at the bridge, University Avenue connects the part of the university property which lies east of the

railroad with the main campus of the university which is situated on the west side of the railroad.

While standing on the bridge, I looked back northwest and recalled the two-storied house with a steeple on top of a turret. That house had been the home of Mr. Billy's parents, Murry Cuthbert and Maud Falkner, in the 1920s. Unlike many southern houses, it was a Gothic architectural design and was built of dark red bricks. It closely resembled Ventress Hall, which was built around 1889. The type of bricks used and the architecture were so similar to the Falkner home as to make it probable that they were built about the same time and designed by the same architect.

When Murry Falkner served as the business manager, later

The Campus Falkner Home
This was the home of Murry C. Falkner and his family when he served as business manager for the university. The house was used by the Delta Psi Fraternity in the 1930s and was demolished in the 1940s. The property is now the site of the Alumni House.

Photo courtesy of Jack Cofield

140

called the financial secretary, of the University of Mississippi from 1918 to 1930, he was privileged to live on the campus in a home provided by the university. It was there that Mr. Billy, his parents, and his brothers, had lived. This house and its surroundings may have helped inspire Mr. Billy to begin writing novels.

I noted that from this house Mr. Billy would have had a view of many of the landmarks which he described in his writings. Usually, but not always, he was able to conceal or obfuscate the identity of the people, events, and places in his writings. Even so, in rare instances I was able to make such identifications of places because they were unique.

In *Sanctuary,* Jefferson, as Mr. Billy described it, could have

Photo courtesy of Herman E. Taylor

Ventress Hall
Built in 1898, Ventress Hall has served as the library, the law school, and the geology building. It was named for the man who introduced the legislation which established the university. In the 1920s, Faulkner painted the roof of the turret when other Oxford painters considered the job too dangerous.

been inspired by no place other than Oxford, Mississippi. Oxford scenes and places were predominant. Mr. Billy placed "Jefferson" a few miles along the railroad from the town of Taylor, Mississippi. About eight miles along the railroad to the south of Oxford, Taylor is one of the few towns or places in Lafayette County which Mr. Billy identified by its actual name in his writings of mythical Yoknapatawpha County.

A unique landmark in Oxford which could be seen from the Falkner home on the campus was the Shack, a two-storied white frame building near the railway station which housed a cafe and had living quarters upstairs. The Shack was the gathering, resting, and visiting place for students, townspeople, and others who waited to catch a train. It appeared in *Sanctuary* as the place where Gowan Stevens got drunk and passed out. Upon awakening, he found that the special student train had left Jefferson. After a wild high speed drive to Taylor, he again missed the train; but found that Temple Drake, an Ole Miss coed, had left the train to join him. Stevens got drunk again and wrecked the car and abandoned Temple near a bootlegger's house and started her on the adventures described in *Sanctuary*. The Shack would have been clearly visible from Mr. Billy's home on the campus, as was the girls' dormitory called the Coop where Temple lived as a coed.

The crest of the ridge upon which the Falkner's house on the campus was situated was the watershed line between the rivers to the north and south. The Cut in the ridge crest beneath the bridge was necessary to lower the track level fifty feet or more for several hundred yards to enable the trains with coal burning engines to cross that elevation of the ridge. The Cut through the ridge, so I had heard, was dug by slaves at the time the railroad was built in the late 1850s. Rain which fell on the south slopes flowed southward to the Yocona River about six miles to the south. If the rain fell on the north side of the ridge it flowed northward to find its way through the windings of little streams to the Tallahatchie River, about twelve miles to the north. The land between the rivers provided the setting, people, events, and inspiration for much of Mr. Billy's writings about his imaginary Yoknapatawpha County.

142

Campus Scenes

When Mr. Billy lived in the house on the campus, it was before most students were allowed to have automobiles on the campus. It was before the roads leading into Oxford and the university were improved enough to encourage anyone to drive to the university from distant points. It was even before the Tri-State Bus Line introduced bus service to Oxford in the 1930s by which one might reach the outside world and those "distant" cities of Memphis, Tennessee, and Jackson, Mississippi.

The railway was then the principal means of transportation. Upon arrival by train at the Oxford station, students often found a considerable problem getting themselves and their baggage to a dormitory room. From the railway station students began a tortuous climb. The incline to the top of the ridge was steep and about four hundred yards of uphill climb along a sidewalk which emerged from the tunnel under the railroad tracks. There it started its circling rise. Except for those who had a dollar to pay to have their trunks and bags carried by waiting students who had rented a truck to capitalize upon this weighty need, the would-be scholars trudged with luggage on their backs and under their arms to the campus of the University of Mississippi.

At campus level this walkway joined the sidewalk which circled the Grove and ran beside a cinder-covered driveway. There before the new student's eyes lay a forest of large oak, gum, hickory, and smaller species of trees, including holly, red bud, maple, and dogwood, in what appeared to be an endless succession as far as one could see. The trees were interspersed with buildings and faculty homes. A Confederate monument stood near the center of the campus and was about three hundred yards west of the bridge. The monument was situated at the principal entrance to the circular drive where many of the academic buildings stood.

New students reaching the top of the ridge would pass the red brick house occupied by the Falkners. From this home it was about a half mile to the student dormitories for men and a few hundred yards to the women's dormitories called the Coop, where the female students, called "chicks," resided. Taylor Hall, a very old brick dormitory for men stood about 200 yards south of the Falkner residence near the Cut. The Falkner home commanded a view of much of the town and campus. The railroad and the bridge across the Cut could be seen from the Falkner's home.

About two hundred yards to the west of the bridge, the road coming from Batesville, Mississippi, then only a dirt road, joined the campus portion of University Avenue. At the southwest corner of the intersection of this road from Batesville with University Avenue there stood an unimposing brick building, which housed the university post office. Inside its door there seemed to be hundreds of small mail boxes. Here the activity heightened when the mail came in, particularly near the first of each month when sacrificing but ambitious parents sent the monthly checks to sons and daugh-

Photo courtesy of Herman E. Taylor

Memorial to the University Grays
The University Grays, a Confederate unit made up solely of students from the University of Mississippi, fought on the Virginia battlefront, and participated in Pickett's Charge. The Grays suffered heavy casualties, and none of the students ever returned to the university. This monument was erected in 1989 by the United Daughters of the Confederacy.

The Lyceum
Built between 1846 and 1848, the Lyceum houses the administrative offices of the university, and was the site of Murry Falkner's office when he served as business manager. During the Civil War, the building was used as a hospital, and in 1962 was the headquarters of the federal forces brought in during the riots that followed the admission of James Meredith to the university.

Photo courtesy of Jack Cofield

ters who might feel themselves to be on the verge of starvation. The mail came in through the night and early morning hours, and it was a matter of extreme importance that it be placed in the boxes before the 10:00 A.M. half-hour break which brought expectant addressees by the hundreds to receive, or inquire about, their mail, or perhaps to buy a two-cent postal card.

Since the morning schedule provided a thirty-minute break at 10:00 A.M., virtually everyone at the university made a trek to the post office for their mail, then down to The Greek's, a restaurant in the building's basement, for a Coke or coffee.

From the classrooms in the Lyceum, Peabody Hall, the medical, education, and engineering schools, from girls' dormitories, athletic fields, and administrative offices, the parade began as the campus bell tolled its tenth reverberating sound. It was a good time for an abbreviated date with coeds who were too much in demand for lengthier courting.

Sometimes the law school stole the show as the senior law students came along wearing black derby hats and ascot ties, and carrying crook-neck canes. With studied dignity they bowed and shook hands with all who looked important, including those they had not seen for as much as an hour. In addition to this throng of young and old, of pompous and humble, of rich and poor, of high or low estate and social caste, of faculty members with greying temples and shiny-seated pants, there was Old Blind Jim and his basket filled with bags of freshly roasted peanuts. For a nickel, one could buy enough peanut morning energy, which, with a nickel Coke, would chase the drowsiness and hunger away for two more hours of classes.

Blind Jim, an ageless Negro who seemed as old when I first saw him as he did the last, was the self-styled "Dean of the Freshman Class." He was a canny soul, who led some cheers at football and baseball games and scarcely ever missed a trip to a far-off game. He knew many students by voice and name and so remained a favorite of several generations, sometimes extending from grandfathers through grandsons, who, upon returning to the campus, would check to see if Blind Jim could recall their names upon hearing their voices.

Amid this varied cavalcade, the beauties of the year displayed their latest styles in dress and physical attractions while their searching eyes surveyed the crowd to see if their future might be discovered there. They were sure that the prettiest and friendliest, who knew the most names and honored all with a wink or smile, would be the likeliest to find her name in the Hall of Fame or elected Miss Ole Miss or have her picture as a "favorite" in *The Ole Miss* yearbook. The power to help designate "the favorites" always got the editor of *The Ole Miss* a special bit of attention from the fairest maidens' eyes.

Such was the environment young William Falkner must have encountered in his employment in the post office as postmaster. Neither long tenure nor a civil service career appears to have been his goal. One version of Mr. Billy's reason for departure from the job

The University Power Plant
This is where Faulkner worked in 1929, hauling coal to feed the furnaces.

was often quoted as: "I refuse to be at the beck and call of every SOB who has two cents with which to buy a postal card." Whether true or not, it has gone the rounds for so long that it must be accorded its place in the Faulkner lore.

In the 1920s Gordon Hall was the principal dormitory for men, and it included the men's dining hall. It stood just north of the baseball field, which played a major role in a story I was told by my friend, Paul Denton, a lawyer in Memphis. The story, confirmed by Johncy Falkner, was that once when Dean Falkner, Mr. Billy's youngest brother, was playing third base in a baseball game between Ole Miss and Mississippi A. and M., Mr. Billy was working as a painter and painting Gordon Hall. Mr. Billy had been drinking whiskey as he watched the game and, as the game progressed, Mr. Billy began yelling at Dean. He attracted considerable attention and as a result was asked to relinquish his position as scoutmaster of the Oxford boy scout troop. Because of this occurrence, Oxford was without a scout troop for several years.

The university post office was about a hundred yards from the power plant. This plant generated the electricity used by the university as well as the steam for heating all buildings on the campus. Here and there on a frosty morning the steam could be seen escaping from the underground pipes of the heat distribution system.

After his marriage in 1929, Mr. Billy got a job at the power plant shoveling coal into the enormous furnace. Train loads of coal were dumped at the south side of the power plant building about a hundred feet away. It was by shovel and wheelbarrow that the coal must be moved to the furnace to provide the energy for the heating and lighting of the buildings of the university.

Mr. Billy probably took the night shift because it would have afforded him more privacy and less visibility to passersby. Here, according to Faulkner legend, when the furnace was amply stoked

The University Power Plant Furnaces According to legend, Faulkner wrote parts of *Sanctuary* and *As I Lay Dying* between trips from the coal pile to the furnaces. The furnaces no longer burn coal, and the great brick smokestack was demolished in the 1980s.

Photo courtesy of Herman E. Taylor

148

with coal, Mr. Billy would turn over the wheelbarrow and use it for a writing surface to complete a page or so of some of his novels.

The Falkners lived in the campus house when I first became conscious of the existence of Mr. Billy. They lived there for about twelve years before the tides of political fortune brought Murry Falkner's replacement as the business manager.

Panorama

Looking to the east from the Falkner home, Mr. Billy would have seen the railway station which served the town and the university. A train station similar to this was described in many of Mr. Billy's books. The station was the center of transportation for the Jefferson and Yoknapatawpha communities. Indeed, since the railroad was almost the only means of access by public transportation to the Oxford and Lafayette County area from the outside world in the 1920s, most people entering or leaving Oxford and the university passed that way.

To the north and west of the railway station was the section house where the section foreman lived. He and his crew of workmen rode up and down the railroad on a little cart, keeping up repairs and replacing rotten cross ties.

Within sight of Mr. Billy's home were also many of the Oxford landmarks such as the railroad siding tracks, the warehouses, coal yards, fuel tanks, and the city power plant, which were depicted in Mr. Billy's books. In the distance, perhaps three-quarters of a mile away, the town clock atop the Lafayette County Courthouse could also be seen, along with the city water tank and the spire of the Episcopal church. Assuming that Yoknapatawpha County was the same as Lafayette County, it would have been in that courthouse that many of Mr. Billy's courtroom scenes took place, including the trials of Lee Goodwin in *Sanctuary* and Mink Snopes in *The Town.* The courthouse is situated in the center of the square and around it swirled the activities of the people of Jefferson and Yoknapatawpha County in Mr. Billy's novels.

The Lafayette County Jail was located a block from the courthouse on North Lamar Boulevard. It, too, was a centerpiece of Mr. Billy's writings, depicted in many of his novels as the Yoknapatawpha Jail. In *Light in August* Joe Christmas, while being taken from the jail to the courthouse for trial, escaped. From this jail in *Sanctuary* Lee Goodwin was taken by a mob and lynched for a murder he had not committed. In *Requiem for a Nun* "that nigger dope fiend whore" was taken from this jail to be hanged. In *The Town* Mink Snopes was held in this jail as he awaited trial. The lynch mob scene in the movie version of *Intruder in the Dust* was filmed at the front of this jail in 1949.

If Mr. Billy had looked south from his home on campus, he could have seen the planing mill, the ice plant, and the oil mill. The ice plant had once been operated by Mr. Billy's father.

To the east of the railroad there were about two hundred acres of university property. This area contained faculty homes and boarding houses for students along Mill Street, (later named Old Taylor Road), University Avenue, and South Depot Street (later named Van Buren Avenue). Even though enrollment in the 1920s was usually less than a thousand students, the university had insufficient facilities for housing and feeding even such a small student enrollment. By the 1980s when the enrollment had greatly increased, the facilities had kept pace and these old houses along University Avenue and Mill Street had been removed.

What is the significance of Ole Miss in a tale of recollections of *Faulkner's Oxford?*

As with a substantial portion of the population of Oxford, the university was probably the magnet which drew Mr. Billy's forebears to settle in Oxford. There had been certain unpleasantries, including the murder of his great-grandfather in Ripley, Mississippi, before the family moved to Oxford. Many of Oxford's residents could trace the cause of their being there to the existence of the university, where one with a large, or growing, family, with aspirations for their education, could introduce his children to the arts, sciences, law, and medicine in preparation for earning a living wherever they might go. Numerous families came to Oxford to educate their children at the university, often returning to their original hometowns after the objectives were accomplished, thus making room for other generations of aspiring scholars in this community where the cost of living was low but where income levels were sometimes even lower. Opportunities for educational achievement were at least available in Oxford.

On that ridge which connects the Ole Miss campus and Oxford between the valleys of the Yocona and Tallahatchie rivers, I was near the center of the sources of Mr. Billy's inspiration to become a writer. Mr. Billy had spent much of his early life in this environment. He had made his permanent home, Rowan Oak, on land which adjoined the university property. When Rowan Oak became a part of the university property it also became one of the most popular campus scenes. Thus, in Mr. Billy's home as well as in his life, a part of Oxford was merged into the University of Mississippi.

Falkner Homes

I crossed the bridge over the railroad and slowly walked along the south side of University Avenue toward the city limits of Oxford. I hoped to refresh my recollection of the times, places, and events which may have been sources of inspiration for Mr. Billy's writings.

About two hundred yards along University Avenue I passed where University High School had been from 1933 to 1963. It had served as a teacher training facility for the School of Education of the University of Mississippi. Its students came from Oxford and the nearby areas of Lafayette County. Mr. Billy's daughter, Jill, attended this school. The school grounds and athletic fields ran south from University Avenue for about six hundred yards to within a few hundred yards of Mr. Billy's home property. Part of the University Woods separated the school grounds from Mr. Billy's home to the southeast on the Old Taylor Road.

The School of Education buildings covered most of the ground along the south side of the avenue where faculty homes and boarding houses had once stood. On the north side of the avenue the former house sites had been made into parking areas.

Continuing along University Avenue for another hundred yards or so, I found myself in front of Memory House, the former home of Johncy Falkner, Mr. Billy's brother. Johncy—John Wesley

Photo courtesy of Herman E. Taylor

Memory House
The home of Johncy Falkner, Memory House was built in 1838 and is one of the
oldest homes in Oxford. It is sometimes called the Ramey-Falkner home.

Thompson Falkner III—also was an author. He had married Lucile
Ramey whose family had owned the property. The house was a
large frame home which dated back to the late 1830s and was said
to be one of the oldest homes in Oxford. The lot was about 150
feet wide. It had a brick walkway leading about two hundred feet
from the avenue to the house. In the 1930s a brick business building had been built in the northeast corner of the yard near University Avenue. A driveway ran from the avenue to the house along
the west boundary of the yard which was also the eastern boundary of the property of the university. In the 1940s the front lawn of
the property was planted with pine seedings and in a few years the
house could hardly be seen from the street.

To the rear of the Ramey-Falkner house was a pasture which
extended south about six hundred feet where it joined the property known as "Brown's Pasture." My friends and I called it Brown's
Pasture because it was owned by J. B. Brown, an Oxford merchant.
The Browns' property, of which this pasture was a part, faced Sec-

ond South Street (South 11th Street). The home was on the south side of Buchanan Avenue, and at an earlier time it had been the home of Mr. Billy's parents.

The pasture land to the west and rear of the Brown home consisted of gullies, steep hills, and small valleys. The pasture joined the property of the University of Mississippi, and south of this pasture lay the land which became Mr. Billy's home called Rowan Oak. North of the western extremity of Brown's Pasture was the land of the home of Johncy Falkner. Brown's Pasture separated the properties of Mr. Billy and Johncy by about two hundred yards.

As a boy, I could scarcely have imagined that in the 1960s my brother Guy B. would own Brown's Pasture and would sell it to the university, enabling the university—which would later acquire Rowan Oak—to increase the land area surrounding Rowan Oak to thirty-two acres, instead of the original fourteen acres. Thus the land of Mr. Billy's home was connected with that of Johncy's former home.

Along the southern boundary of the former Brown's Pasture there was a ditch which had no flowing stream in it except after heavy rains. My friends and I called it "Stink Creek" because it drained much of the town's sewage.

This pasture land had provided a place for baseball games. Between the back fence of Johncy's property and Stink Creek was a small level area which included enough flat land for a baseball field, if the right fielder and left fielder were willing to run down hill to catch the balls. Stink Creek lay behind the catcher. A tipped ball, foul, or miss by the catcher would require the retrieval of the ball from Stink Creek. The ball could be retrieved from the sewage with a stick and then rolled around in the dirt until it was dry enough to play with again. After all grew tired of fishing balls out of the sewage, the games were moved up the hill to the south to the level plateau which lay west of Mr. Billy's house and garden.

One day while playing near Stink Creek the game came to a sudden halt. A three-motored airplane flew over. With such excitement in the skies the ballgame between the Ragged Ass Ramblers of Lake Street and the Second South Streeters was temporarily sus-

Photo courtesy of Herman E. Taylor

The Home of Miss Elma Meek
The home contains the apartment which Faulkner and Miss Estelle rented after their marriage in 1929. The home is now owned by Howard Duvall, Jr.

pended to allow everyone to marvel at that flying machine. None of the players had ever seen a three-motored plane before.

After the baseball games were moved up to the plateau, Mr. Billy would sometimes come out and squat near first base to watch the game. Usually he just squatted and smoked his pipe, occasionally speaking to those who came near when they got on first base.

About a quarter of a mile farther east from the Ramey-Falkner home along University Avenue, I saw the two-story white frame home on the north side of the street which in 1929 had been that of Miss Elma Meek. The house was situated on ground which was high up a steep bank, made higher when University Avenue had been graded down for paving in the late 1920s. The bank rose about fifteen feet above the sidewalk on the west side of her lawn. This house was where Mr. Billy and Miss Estelle lived after they were married in 1929 and where he may have done some of his writing. I recalled seeing Mr. Billy returning home in the early morning hours dressed in his work clothes as I delivered the *Com-*

The Home of Murry C. and Maud Falkner
This is the home that was built for William Faulkner's parents after "The Big Place" was moved to make room for it. It is now owned by Dean Faulkner Wells, William Faulkner's niece.

mercial Appeal. Probably he was returning from his job at the university power plant.

Moving along east on University Avenue, I came to the corner of South 11th Street. On the southeast corner of its intersection with University Avenue had stood the big three-story frame house which had once been the home of Mr. Billy's grandfather, John Wesley Thompson Falkner, at one time the bank president, who is believed by many to have been one of the inspirations for Mr. Billy's novel *Sartoris,* which depicted a banker's family which bore some resemblance to the Falkner family. Sometimes this was called the Big Place by members of the Falkner family.

As I rounded the corner of University Avenue and South Lamar I passed the home built by Mr. Murry and Miss Maud Falkner in about 1930. I recalled how, after the house was completed and they had moved in, they had played cards with Justice of the Peace and Mrs. P. B. Furr on the front porch on many summer evenings.

Photo courtesy of Herman E. Taylor

The Home of John Wesley Thompson Falkner
The home of William Faulkner's uncle stands at the corner of South Lamar Boulevard and Filmore Avenue.

In the wintertime they had moved inside where they could be seen through the large window of their living room shuffling and dealing cards. The Furrs were their next door neighbors to the south. I suspected that this may have inspired Mr. Billy to describe a similar scene in *Light in August* when Joe Christmas walked the streets of the town after committing a murder.

Across the street to the east of the Falkner house was a single-story stuccoed house atop a knoll in which Murry and Maud had lived when their sons were growing up. Johncy Falkner has described this in his book *My Brother Bill* as the site where he and his brothers built and tried to fly an airplane from the hilltop to the east over a big gully.

Along the front sidewalk of the Murry C. Falkner home, there was a concrete wall about one to two feet high. Originally, when the Big Place faced South Lamar, there was a wrought iron fence affixed in this concrete wall. At the entrance to the walkway which once led to the front door of the Big Place I could see the name

Falkner molded in the concrete, and I noticed that the *N* was imprinted in the concrete backwards. This reminded me of Mr. Billy's description of the sign on the Snopes Hotel in *Sartoris* in which the *S* was printed backward.

Barnstorming

In the early 1930s barnstormers flew biplanes around the town and countryside, charging $2.50 for a ride. These barnstorming aviators gave lessons in flying for ten dollars. They had excited the imagination of all smaller boys and many older men such as Mr. Billy and his brothers. It was about the time when movies showed such films as *Hell's Angels* and *Lilac Time* about the flying aces of World War I.

My friends and I were almost overcome with desire to have a ride in an airplane after spending many Sunday afternoons watching the take-offs and landings, first in Mr. Alvis's pasture about a mile south of the Oxford city limits on Highway 7, then in the creek bottom which drained much of the campus of the university. On one occasion so many people wanted to take a ride that the pilots called Memphis to send down another plane to accommodate the crowd. It was truly a great occasion an hour or so later when someone pointed to a speck in the northern sky as being the other plane arriving.

At a later time the plateau land on Temple's Farm, a half mile nearer to the town (present location of the Lafayette County Hospital), was made into the municipal airport. It had two runways of graded and smoothed red clay dirt, one running north and south and a second running to the northeast. Each was about five hundred yards in length. That length was sufficient for the take-offs and landings of the old biplanes.

There were moments of high drama, as when one biplane in landing flipped over and came to rest bottom side upward, yet Mr. Alvin Hipp, a mail carrier, and another passenger were able to walk away from the plane, unhurt but thoroughly unnerved.

Once after a heavy rain, the field was still muddy, and the plane became splattered from nose to tail with mud, which turned it a brownish color all over the fuselage. The chief barnstormer pilot was named Captain Verne Omlie. He told several of the smaller boys, including me, that if we would clean the mud off, he would give us a *free* ride. This was a greater opportunity than anyone had even hoped for. Almost in unison the other boys and I accepted the proposition. There were no water hoses which could be used in cleaning up the plane, but there was a nearby water faucet close to the buildings used for the exhibits when the county fair was held. We boys found buckets and old rags and carried the water and swabbed and rinsed and rubbed and cleaned with considerable motivation, while Captain Verne watched the work until he was satisfied.

Then came the time for each to fly.

Captain Verne was more than generous in his compensation for the work. He took each pair of boys up for at least a half hour. I got more than I had expected, bargained for, or wanted.

After the novelty of seeing my town, its streets, and homes, the square, and other familiar scenes from these strangely vertical angles, the new began to wear off. Perhaps for his own entertainment or perhaps intending to give me something to remember about my first flight, Captain Omlie gave me some flying time that would never be forgotten.

This was in the days when biplanes could and did do things which would be impossible with faster flying machines. Building up speed, Verne would suddenly turn the plane nose up and do a complete flip and come down into level flight again. Then he would almost do the same thing, but instead he would drive the plane upward until it stalled and fell off to the side into a heart-stopping tailspin, which he would let continue until it seemed that the plane was certain to crash into the ground. Just barely before the impending crash, he would zoom out of the spin and start his climb again. Upon attaining sufficient altitude he would come down in a power dive, again pulling out of it just in time to keep from hitting the ground. Then Captain Verne would go flying along at increasing speeds and would climb as though he were going to do another flip, but as the plane lost its speed in the climb, he would let it fall off over to the side and circle round and round in tight little looping circles until the plane was almost exactly at the end of the landing runway where he leveled out and made a perfect landing. I was surprised to find myself still alive.

Woozily I took off the helmet and goggles I had worn to fend off the wind and the rushing air. I simply oozed out of the cockpit and somehow found the ground. With unsteady steps and lurching a bit I went over to a shady spot and fell down feeling that the earth itself was heading for another tailspin.

By now the afternoon was moving on, and I thought I had better be getting home and started toward the road. As I rounded the corner of a building, I almost ran squarely into Mr. Billy. He was hurrying along, seemingly in the hope of getting in some flying time before twilight came. In his hand was his flying helmet, complete with flying goggles of his own. By now it was generally known that he was taking lessons from Captain Verne, and it was well remembered that he had once been in the Royal Canadian Air Force. He did not pause and scarcely spoke, and I had the feeling that he had hardly noticed me, so intent was he upon what was going on near the plane.

The Falkner boys, William, Johncy, and Dean, took to flying as might fish to water. Johncy and Dean kept their interest active in the sport of flying, even engaged in the business of operating a flying service, and owned a plane or two. Flying would take a heavy toll from these early flyers. The great risks in barnstorming and stunt flying made accidents a likely occurrence.

I was going home from the golf course late one Sunday afternoon in 1935 and turned from University Avenue through the service station which occupied the southwest corner of its juncture with South Lamar. The station was on land which had once been part of the yard of the old Falkner home where Mr. Billy's grandfather had lived. I sensed that something strange was going on next door at the home of Mr. Billy's mother, Miss Maud.

Then I was told by someone at the service station that Dean Falkner had been killed in a plane crash. Only a day or so before, I had seen Dean and his pretty bride going to and from that house. I walked slowly on past the house trying not to stare while feeling a deep sense of sorrow.

Mr. Billy had written *Sartoris* in 1929. In that book he appeared to have premonitions as he described the adventuresome and reckless natures of the Sartoris twins, both of whom had been killed in plane crashes. Mr. Billy and Johncy looked almost like twins to me, but they escaped the fate which Dean encountered.

Johncy, however, was disabled in a plane accident during World War II. Captain Verne Omlie, who had been the Falkners' flying instructor, perished in a plane crash near St. Louis in 1937.

Lake Street Rambling

Intending to revisit my former home on Lake Street, I had paused to reflect upon my surroundings. Then I realized that I had been standing for several minutes on the corner of South Lamar and Filmore Avenue in front of the home of Mr. Billy's Uncle John, that is, John Wesley Thompson Falkner, attorney at law. I was across South Lamar from the site of the former Oldham home as I contemplated the changes which had taken place. The Oldham home was gone. The only familiar things I could recognize were two of the oak trees between the sidewalk and the curb of the street. All across the front of the former Oldham lawn now stood the building of the South Central Bell Telephone Company. The oaks had been a few inches in diameter in 1924 when I had observed the reunion of Mr. Billy and Miss Estelle. Now the trunks of the trees were a foot or so in diameter. The sites of the homes which had formerly stood on the east side of South Lamar had been turned into commercial property all of the way north to University Avenue.

South along South Lamar, however, the homes appeared much the same as they had looked when I was a boy.

As I slowly moved along, preoccupied in reminiscence, I came to the intersection of South Lamar and Lake Street, although the street sign now read Buchanan Avenue.

I turned to the east and suddenly felt transported back to my youth as I passed beneath the limbs of the large magnolia tree which still stood in the center of the lawn of the J. E. Neilson home. I remembered how I had once rolled up the dried petals of the magnolia blossoms and attempted smoking them when I was about fourteen years of age.

Lake Street had originally run to the east and south for about a mile from its intersection with South Lamar Boulevard. In earlier times, probably throughout the nineteenth century, this had been a busy road leading to the southeast part of the county. About a half-mile along Lake Street, an old abandoned road branched off at what became South 16th Street and Johnson Avenue and led down a steep, gullied trail. This road ran past the old Chilton-Haley house, said to be one of the oldest houses in town, having been built in 1832. The old trail ran below the hill to the south just outside of the city, where the hangman had once done his chores and hanged both a white man and a Negro for the murder of a deputy sheriff and a revenue agent. The officers had been killed when they approached the murderer's whiskey still.

The old roadway had descended about a hundred feet below the hills to the south and west before it crossed Birney's Branch. The abandoned roadbed crossed the small stream at a ford. Some old tales claim that Oxford got its name because oxen forded the shallow branch at this point. Others insist that the town was named for Oxford, England.

East of Birney's Branch can be seen traces of the old road where, for a long period of time, the wagon wheels had cut into the red clay and sandy subsoil, and erosion by wind and rain had carried dust and mud away, leaving deep scars and depressions in the hillsides.

Downstream, about three hundred yards south of the ford, a swift spring-fed stream flowed into Birney's Branch. This stream was just north of an Indian mound. Mr. Murry Falkner and his sons hiked to this area on Sunday afternoons to wade in the branch and hunt for Indian arrowheads, according to Johncy's writing in *My Brother Bill.* I had once found an arrowhead on that Indian mound.

When the Falkner boys and their father had walked down Lake Street they had passed the iron picket fence of the Thompson-Chandler home facing what became South 13th Street. This home and the members of that family made a lasting impression on the

The Chandler Home

According to Johncy Falkner, this is the home that inspired William Faulkner to write *The Sound and the Fury.* Construction on the house was begun in 1860, but was interrupted by the Civil War.

boys. Johncy Falkner wrote that these walks past the Chandlers' house inspired Mr. Billy to write *The Sound and the Fury.*

The Chandler home faced South 13th Street and was between Buchanan and Johnson avenues. It had been built for William Thompson by William Turner in about 1860. This house fascinated me since I had been born across the street on Johnson Avenue. I vividly remembered the Chandler home because I passed it daily during my youth. It was bounded on the west along the sidewalk of South 13th Street by a cast iron fence made of four-foot-high iron pickets encased in an iron frame and anchored in concrete. This fence had surrounded the county courthouse, before the courthouse had been almost destroyed by Yankee troops in 1864. The top of the pickets stood six to eight feet above the sidewalk. The sidewalk was lower than the level of the Chandlers' yard. The house itself was a white two-story building of frame and clapboard construction and of Greek Revival architectural design. It had four

The Tate House

Situated on Johnson Avenue, this home may have inspired the "square paintless house with its rotting portico" that was the Compson home of *The Sound and the Fury.* The site is now a residential subdivision.

columns which rose about twenty-four feet to support the roof of the porch.

To the north of the Chandler house the land dropped steeply into ravines behind the house on South Lamar, including that of Major L. E. Oldham, Mr. Billy's father-in-law.

To the south there was a view of the countryside and distant horizon, but the view was partly obscured by a large oak tree in the front yard of the home of Mrs. Guy B. Taylor, my widowed mother.

Attached to the rear of the Chandler house was a cottage and other rooms which predated the front of the house. A side view of the house from my home gave the impression that the front part of the house was too tall and too thin in appearance. To the east and behind the house were the quarters of the servants, the chicken house, and a small barn. To the rear of the buildings was a pasture of about two acres for the cows. Along the south boundary of the

Chandler home fronting along Johnson Avenue, there was a strip of land of about an acre which was usually planted in corn or other vegetables. From the street level, honeysuckle vines covered the bank which rose about six or eight feet to the level of the field. This house was said to have been occupied by Yankee troops during the Civil War, and an attempt by the Yankees to burn it down failed when the fire was extinguished by the servants.

I did not disagree with Johncy Falkner in his belief that the Chandler house was the one which had stirred Mr. Billy to write about in *The Sound and the Fury.* On the other hand, I was not so sure that the Chandler house was the one described by Mr. Billy as the Compson home. I believe that he described the Carter-Tate house as the Compson home.

The Tate house was the home of the Henry L. Tate family and was situated in the 1400 and 1500 blocks of Johnson Avenue, southeast of the Chandler home. It is sometimes described as the Carter-Tate home. It was a two-story house of frame construction and had weathered wood columns at the north side and west side entrance porticos. It was covered with wood siding. The Tate house appeared never to have been painted on the outside. It was built in an *L* shape but appeared to be square when viewed from the north and west. In such matters as age, architecture, design, elevation, acreage, and view, it outdid the Chandler home.

In the last chapter of *The Sound and the Fury* Mr. Billy described the Compson home where Benji and Jason lived as "the square paintless house with its rotting portico." I believed that this description more nearly fitted the Tate house than it did the Chandler house. I could recall no time when the Chandler house was "paintless" or had a "rotting portico." The Chandler house was not "square."

Mr. Billy was very familiar with the older homes on Lake Street. Most of these homes were on several acres of land and resembled small farms.

While visiting my mother in the 1940s, my sister and I were swinging on my mother's front porch when Mr. Billy drove around the corner toward town in his 1935 Ford touring car with the top down and a large wire chicken coop protruding from the trunk of

The Home of Mrs. Guy B. Taylor, Sr.
Located on Johnson Avenue, this home is believed to have been built in 1866. In 1961, Mrs. Taylor sold a flock of her chickens to William Faulkner, which he "personally caught, caged, loaded, and hauled away."

his car. Many years later, about 1961, Mr. Billy acquired a flock of chickens from my mother, Mrs. Guy B. Taylor. She described the transaction as follows:

> At one time William and John had a farm out in the country, and John and his wife Lucile lived out there. I was raising Buff Orpingtons then. Often Estelle (William's wife) would walk over to my house to buy eggs to take to the farm. I wondered why they didn't raise their own chickens. At that time everyone in Oxford was raising his own chickens. Sometimes William and Estelle would drive by in their car to get eggs (they always rode in an old, battered car when they could have afforded the best one manufactured) and we had a pleasant chat. And often William drove by my place to get the granddaughter of a Negro minister who lived on the edge of town. He would take her to his big old home near mine to play with his little girl Jill. She had

plenty of white children her own age to play with, but I suppose William wanted her also to know little colored girls.

A few years ago my granddaughter returned from Southern Rhodesia because of the fighting there. She visited me with her three children—a girl of seven, a boy of five, and Beth, the baby of two, who looked like a doll, pretty and babylike. At about that time I decided to go out of the chicken business. I placed an ad in *The Oxford Eagle* and offered my fine Buff Orpingtons for sale. A short while after the paper came out, William Faulkner drove over in a truck to buy the chickens. He had on old clothes; he never did dress up much when he was out working. He had a Negro boy with him, and he had brought a coop, but he did most of the work, and in a short time had shooed the chickens into the coop and driven off.

But he had taken the time to admire and talk to Baby Beth. "Grandmother," my elder granddaughter said, "you could become famous by selling your chickens to Mr. Faulkner!"*

The granddaughter referred to by Mrs. Taylor was Mary Ann Taylor Donaldson (Mrs. Frank R.) of Auburndale, Massachusetts. She and Dr. Donaldson have served as medical missionaries for several years.

Antebellum Homes

On the ridge to the west of South Lamar is the highest elevation within the city of Oxford. At the highest point of the ridge, the former home of Jacob Thompson, one of the early settlers and large landowners in Oxford and Lafayette County, had been built. He once served as congressman for the district and as secretary of

*Reprinted with the permission of the Louisiana State University Press from *William Faulkner of Mississippi,* edited by James W. Webb and A. Wigfall Green. Copyright 1965 by Louisiana State University Press.

Photo courtesy of Herman E. Taylor

Shadowlawn
Built in 1857, this was the home of William Smith Neilson, a leading merchant of Oxford, and is now owned by William Lewis, Jr. Many Faulkner scholars believe this to be the home described in "A Rose for Emily."

the interior in President Buchanan's cabinet. The original Jacob Thompson home was destroyed by Yankee troops during the Civil War. Later the house was rebuilt and in time became the Elliot home and in the 1960s the home of Dr. Beckett Howorth, Jr. A widespread supposition is that the Thompson family may have been depicted as the Compson family in Mr. Billy's writings about the town of Jefferson.

This ridge to the west of South Lamar runs west to the Jacob Thompson house and ends at the Old Taylor Road about two hundred yards to the south of the entrance gate of Mr. Billy's home, Rowan Oak.

The influence of family, friends, social caste, and wealth seems to have been important in the design and building of the great old columned frame antebellum homes. In the book entitled *Faulkners, Fortunes and Flames,* Jack Case Wilson relates that Jacob Thompson allowed his gardener to design and construct the

Photo courtesy of Herman E. Taylor

Ammadelle
Built between 1856 and 1866 for the Thomas Pegues family, it later became the
home of the Bem Price, Minnie Sivley, David G. Neilson, and John Tatum families.

brickwork terraces around the large magnolia tree on the lawn of
the neighboring Shegog home, known as Rowan Oak after it became the home of William Faulkner. He also states that the Jacob
Thompson gardener made plantings of magnolia trees in front of
the home of William Thompson, Jacob's brother. That home later
became known as the Chandler home on Lake Street (South 13th
Street).

One other columned antebellum home in the south of Oxford is
the William S. Neilson home, now called Shadowlawn. It is situated
on the southwest corner of South 11th Street and Filmore Avenue.
William S. Neilson, who built this home, was the founder of the
J. E. Neilson Company, Oxford's oldest retail business.

The William S. Neilson home, the Carter-Tate home, and Rowan
Oak included two columned porticos, one on the front and one on
a side.

In terms of grandeur and permanence, these woodframe homes
pale when compared with the brick mansion house called Am-

The Isom, Morris, and Worthy Home

Built in the early 1840s by Dr. I. D. Isom, some scholars believe that this, and not Shadowlawn, was the inspiration for "A Rose for Emily." J. H. "Jody" Morris, a sewing machine salesman who lived here may have inspired Faulkner's character Ratliff, who was also a sewing machine salesman.

madelle built 1856-1866 on North Lamar Boulevard by William Turner for the Thomas Pegues family. Later it became in succession the Price, Sivley, David Neilson, and Tatum home. It was featured in the movie version of Mr. Billy's novel *Home from the Hills.*

In the late 1930s, Mr. David G. Neilson, grandson of William S. Neilson, bought Ammadelle and about fifteen acres of the land surrounding it.

The Isom, Morris, and Worthy home, situated on Jefferson Avenue (formerly Cemetery Street) west of North 11th Street, is listed in the National Registry of Historic Places. It was built in 1843-44. The house has six large solid wood columns along the front of the veranda. It is of frame construction and has five large windows which go down nearly to the veranda floor and five more windows on the second floor. The property was acquired by Dr.

and Mrs. H. D. Worthy in 1960, and they restored it to excellent condition.

This house is thought by some Faulkner scholars to have been the inspiration for the writing of "A Rose for Emily" which Mr. Billy published in 1934. Other, and probably most Faulkner scholars, believe the story was written about Shadowlawn, the William S. Neilson home. Faulkner described the home of Emily as being on a street on which a cotton gin and service station were situated. No service station or cotton gin has ever been situated on South 11th Street. There was a gin and service station at the intersection of Jefferson Avenue and North Lamar in the 1920s.

I wondered if Mr. Billy had inserted the reference to the service station and cotton gin on what had been one of the best streets in Oxford to divert attention from Shadowlawn as the site about which "A Rose for Emily" was written.

Conflicts of the Heart

It appeared to me that all of these great old houses represented the *nouveau riche* "cotton aristocracy" of the pre-Civil War period from about 1835 to 1860 in Mississippi. They had prospered mightily for about twenty-five years, principally from growing cotton. They had acquired the land at little cost from the Indians, or from the government, and with slave labor, they had become "the establishment," at least for a time. Many of the prewar wealthy suffered a decline of as much as 90 percent in wealth in the period from 1860 to 1870, according to *The Heritage of Lafayette County, Mississippi, Volume I.* Thereafter the debacle in affluence continued for decades through Reconstruction, economic depressions, yellow fever epidemics, and the restructuring of the economic, political, and social order.

Some established themselves elsewhere. Jacob Thompson, former congressman and cabinet member, who, having salvaged considerable wealth by depositing some of his funds in England during the Civil War, left the town and county and established a new domicile in Memphis, Tennessee.

The hill farm land of Lafayette County had been denuded of

its topsoil, and erosion permanently reduced the agricultural productiveness of that land. Without slave labor it was sometimes impracticable to cultivate the large acreages of land held by the once-affluent landowners. Land values plummeted, and it became possible for previously unlanded, poor, and uneducated whites to acquire land and to try to make a living by farming. Often these attempts proved unsuccessful and for the ensuing generations the migration from farm lands of hill country like that of Lafayette County continued and accelerated. Such migrants may have included the Snopeses of Mr. Billy's novels *Sartoris, The Hamlet, The Town,* and *The Mansion.* By their number and the intensity of their aspirations, the Snopesian kind were destined to supplant the establishment of Sartorises, Sutpens, Greniers and their kind who had achieved such economic and social position as they had possessed by acquiring great landholdings and building transient economic power by the labor of the slave.

Without slaves, owners of large holdings could not hold onto the land, and slavery was no more: that is, of course, slavery as it had existed. In an economic sense, slavery would continue. The poor might elevate themselves by exploiting those who were even poorer, or by manipulating governmental power and legal systems for their greatest benefit, and by denying the former slave the right to vote and to gain education at public expense and other so-called "civil rights."

I was curious as to whether Mr. Billy was seeking to accomplish some lofty purpose, some philosophical goal, some expiation of his frustrations in writing of his town, county, and region in terms which could have applications to the entire South, and I posed these questions to myself:

What inspired Mr. Billy to write of the people, places, and events of his own habitat? Did Mr. Billy aspire to change, or merely to explain, the social, economic, and political quagmire in which the South found itself for much of the century following the Civil War? Did Mr. Billy favor or resent the rising power of the previously unlanded white and black populations as they were freed from the tyrannies of the agricultural system which had resembled that of feudal Europe? Was he troubled by the demise of the landed aristocracy all over the South who, without slave labor, had been unable to continue holding great acreages of land?

I had heard the Civil War described as "a rich man's war," and reluctantly and uneasily found myself considering this enigma: Had the Civil War been fought by the white portion of the population of the South to keep its black population enslaved for the benefit, primarily, of owners of slaves?

Was Mr. Billy subtly expressing his own feelings concerning the South when in *Absalom, Absalom,* his character Quentin Compson protested repeatedly, "I don't hate it," referring to the South?

Was the preservation of the slave holding establishment the "just and holy cause" as proclaimed upon the Confederate monument near the south side of the courthouse on the square in Oxford? Mr. Billy, in writing *Requiem for a Nun,* noted that the Confederate soldier atop the monument was not staring toward the north and the enemy, but stared toward the South. Then he posed the questions as to whether the soldier was looking for reinforcements, or for deserters, or for a safe place to run. Did Mr. Billy's ridicule disclose his disdain for the southern "cause?"

Mr. Billy's biographer, Joseph Blotner, in his book entitled *Faulkner: A Biography,* noted that Mr. Billy had once identified himself as being Quentin Compson.

I recalled that Mr. Billy, in accepting the Nobel Prize in Stockholm in 1950, had said:

> . . . the problems of the human heart in conflict with itself, which alone can make good writing because only that is worth writing about. . . .

I wondered whether Mr. Billy had in mind his own feelings of ambivalent love and hate for the South, its customs and peoples when he spoke of the "human heart in conflict with itself."

I suspected that I had been led by Mr. Billy's inner conflicts when, in reading many of his novels, I had found myself alternating between admiration and disgust.

It seemed probable to me that Mr. Billy's conflicts within his own heart may have created some of his greatest inspirations.

172

Chapter 10

Fear

In the spring of 1951 I heard that Mr. Billy was going to give the commencement address at the graduation exercises of University High School. His daughter Jill was a member of that class, and she was able to persuade him to make this address. I had never heard of Mr. Billy making a speech in Oxford. Thus I felt compelled to attend to see and hear Mr. Billy's performance.

The graduation exercises for University High School were held on the university campus in Fulton Chapel on May 28, 1951. The chapel had a stage large enough for seating all of the members of the graduating class and the speakers who were on the program.

When Nina Claire and I arrived at the chapel, we found that the crowd had almost filled the chapel, but we were able to find seats in the balcony. From that point we had difficulty in hearing all that was said on the stage, but we were able to hear most of it, that is, until it came time for Mr. Billy's speech.

Some ladies who sat near us were overheard saying that people from all over the world would give almost anything for an opportunity to hear his address, that those who had seats were very lucky people. The air of expectancy heightened as the time drew near for Mr. Billy to speak. When he was introduced he came unhurriedly to the podium. He wasted no time with introductory remarks, jokes, or recognitions of important personages, as gradu-

173

ation speakers sometimes do. Instead, he launched directly into his subject matter.

The acoustics were poor in the chapel and the public address system did not amplify Mr. Billy's voice to the point of being readily understandable. He spoke softly in a low-pitched voice, and the crowd became very quiet as most were trying to hear every word he spoke.

While I understood most of what Mr. Billy said, I was greatly relieved when I discovered that *The Oxford Eagle's* reporter had gotten the complete speech, and it was published in that newspaper on May 31, 1951 as follows:

Never Be Afraid

Years ago, before any of you were born, a wise Frenchman said, "If youth knew; if age could." We all know what he meant: that when you are young, you have the power to do anything, but you don't know what to do. Then, when you have got old, and experience and observation have taught you answers, you are tired, frightened; you don't care, you want to be left alone as long as you yourself are safe; you no longer have the capacity or the will to grieve over any wrongs but your own.

So you young men and women in this room tonight, and in thousands of other rooms like this one about the earth today, have the power to change the world, rid it forever of war and injustice and suffering, provided you know how, know what to do. And so according to the old Frenchman, since you can't know what to do because you are young, then anyone standing here with a head full of white hair, should be able to tell you.

But maybe this one is not as old and wise as his white hairs pretend or claim. Because he can't give you a glib answer or pattern either. But he can tell you this, because he believes this. What threatens us today is fear. Not the atom bomb, nor even fear of it, because if the bomb fell on Oxford tonight, all it could do would be to kill us, which is nothing, since in doing that, it will have robbed itself of its only power over us: which is fear of it, the being afraid of it.

Our danger is not that. Our danger is the forces in the world today which are trying to use man's fear to rob him of his individuality, his soul, trying to reduce him to an unthinking mass by fear and bribery—giving him free food which he has not earned, easy and valueless money which he has not worked for;—the economies or ideologies or political systems, communist or socialist or democratic, whatever they wish to call themselves, the tyrants and the politicians, American or European or Asiatic, whatever they call themselves, who would reduce man to one obedient mass for their own aggrandisement and power, or because they themselves are baffled and afraid, afraid of, or incapable of, believing in man's capacity for courage and endurance and sacrifice.

"That is what we must resist, if we are to change the world for man's peace and security. It is not men in the mass who can and will save Man. It is Man himself, created in the image of God so that he shall have the power and the will to choose right from wrong, and so be able to save himself because he is worth saving;—Man, the individual, men and women, who will refuse always to be tricked or frightened or bribed into surrendering, not just the right but the duty too, to choose between justice and injustice, courage and cowardice, sacrifice and greed, pity and self;—who will believe always not only in the right of man to be free of injustice and rapacity and deception, but the duty and responsibility of Man to see that justice and truth and pity and compassion are done.

"So, never be afraid. Never be afraid to raise your voice for honesty and truth and compassion, against injustice and lying and greed. If you, not just you in this room tonight, but in all the thousands of other rooms like this one about the world today and tomorrow and next week, will do this, not as a class or classes, but as individuals, men and women, you will change the earth. In one generation all the Napoleons and Hitlers and Caesars and Mussolinis and Stalins and all the other tyrants who want power and aggrandizement, and the simple politicians and time-servers

175

who themselves are merely baffled or ignorant or afraid, who have used, or are using, or hope to use, man's fear and greed for man's enslavement, will have vanished from the face of it."

Chapter 11

Conundrums

In 1955 change was in the air. The Korean Conflict like all wars, finally ended. Armed standoff ruled the 38th parallel in Korea, which was a "no man's land." It had ended in victory, defeat, or stalemate, depending upon one's perspective and predilections. A more major war with China had barely been averted by President Truman's restraint of General MacArthur before the Yalu River was crossed. The veterans who had survived that war had returned to their homes and towns, or had relocated and reentered civilian society, alongside the veterans of World War II who, by now, were graying around the temples and fathering families of increasing size and finding their places in the establishment.

Society in America had been restructured in 1954 by the U.S. Supreme Court when it decided the case of *Brown v. Board of Education of Topeka* (and Virginia and Delaware). The court found that separate schools for blacks and whites were inherently violative of the equal protection clause of the Fourteenth Amendment to the Constitution. It decreed that public schools must be integrated with due deliberate speed under the supervision of the federal courts.

Why, I wondered, did it take eighty-seven years after the adoption of the fourteenth Amendment to the Constitution, for the U.S. Supreme Court to discover that its "equal protection clause" was violated by a state maintaining separate schools for blacks and whites?

Many battles were yet unfought concerning the scope and nature of racial integration, not the least of which would occur in Oxford and on the Ole Miss campus in 1962.

James Meredith, a Negro, would insist upon his right to become a member of the student body of the University of Mississippi. With the help of President John F. Kennedy, the federal courts, and 30,000 troops of the federal government, he would be able to prove that his point was legally correct. While battles would rage for many years to come, the major issue had been decided. The Negro was entitled to equal protection of the law in acquiring an education. The Old South was in for change in almost every one of its institutions, customs, and thoughts. When viewed in comparison with the great social upheavals of the past, the Civil Rights Revolution might be classified as a relatively peaceful revolution in terms of loss of life and destruction of property values. Only two lives were lost in the Ole Miss battle. James Meredith would attend and graduate from Ole Miss. Two decades later he would be invited back to the campus as an honored alumnus.

There were some members of the local business establishment who even foresaw the possibilities of advantage in such a change. One merchant observed—in private conversation, of course, and fortified by a couple of beers to the point of expression of profound insight—that "business would be a hell of a lot better if that half of the population which is black should be educated to the point of being able to earn a decent wage."

In 1955, I returned to Oxford after having been away for about four years during and after the Korean Conflict. I had been recalled to active duty in the army the day I had graduated from law school. I later learned how it happened that I had been recalled to active duty. Some old "friends" of mine, who had served with me in the Sixth Signal Company during World War II, were in key positions in the Pentagon during the Korean Conflict. They later admitted to me that they had seen my name on a list of reserve officers, and they thought it funny to imagine seeing my expression when I got the word that I was being recalled to duty.

Prior to my recall by the Army, I had been active in the Oxford Junior Chamber of Commerce, which had tried to bring an industry to Oxford. The Jaycees had not been very selective regarding the type or size of the industry, for almost any industry would offer jobs for the unemployed and a payroll which might stimulate business all over town. They had seriously considered constructing a factory building as bait for some industry which might wish to relocate in Oxford. In fact, I had worked on the project up until the time I left Oxford to reenter the military service.

Now I was happy to be back home and had long anticipated getting old Rebel, my liver and white bird dog, now about ten years old, in the car with me to go for a little exploration of the fields, grasslands, and thickets near the edge of town. Although the season for hunting birds was over, I thought there was a possibility of finding a covey of quail and once more enjoying Rebel's point before flushing them into the whir of wings which I thought must be one of the most exciting events of a hunter's life. Old Rebel instantly understood when he saw me in hunting clothes and jumped into the car happily awaiting an adventure. From nearly forgotten habit, I turned the car toward South Lamar, and then to Garfield Avenue and west a few blocks.

The houses and trees looked unchanged since my high school days about twenty years before, except for a new house or two on land which then had been playing fields or pastures.

As I slowly moved along, it occurred to me that while I had been away, a new factory had come to town and that it was reputed to be quite large, prosperous, and modern. It was almost "heavy" industry, being engaged in manufacturing gas or electric ranges and other appliances, and it employed several hundred workers. My mind returned to the campaigns the Jaycees had tried to launch to interest the city fathers, politicians, bankers, and merchants in attracting such a plant, and my curiosity grew.

I turned left into the widening curve where Garfield Avenue became the Old Taylor Road, near the woods where once I had almost been detected by Mr. Billy when I had shot at a squirrel. As I straightened the wheels I noticed that a man and a dog were walking on the west side of the road and coming north. I noticed that the man was looking off into the distance above and beyond the car as if he neither knew or wanted to know who might be in the car.

The man wore a floppy felt hat which was pulled down well on his head, and the brim was turned down in front and back. He wore baggy flannel pants and a brown tweed coat. The pipe in his mouth and the moustache above his upper lip seemed very familiar. I recognized this man as Mr. Billy Faulkner. I hit the brakes, skidded to a stop, and bolted out to speak. I had not seen Mr. Billy in several years and advanced enthusiastically with an extended hand and spoke. Mr. Billy greeted me as casually as if we had met the day before. "Hello, Herman. How are you?"

It was probable that Mr. Billy did not even know that I had been away from Oxford for about four years. In small towns, where things follow pretty much the same routine, it is possible for days to turn into weeks, months, and years, and for years to pass almost unnoticed unless there are important and unusual events by which to mark their passing or to distinguish one from the next. Such sameness may be one of the pleasures of small town living, because people know what to expect.

While in the army I could usually account for time by such events as a change of station, the date of the last visit home, or that of my last promotion or other major events. Not so with the local folks who scarcely know of the presence or absence of their fellow townsmen unless they are needed in some way. Thus they may have no consciousness of other people's departures or returns or doings in between.

This impression was firmly planted in my mind on one occasion when in Oxford I chanced to visit a store near the square which I had frequented in my college years. I had not seen or spoken to the business manager of that store in approximately fifteen years. The manager had, of course, spent those years checking credit, sending bills, and collecting accounts. When I approached the office where the manager was busily examining some papers, he barely raised his head so his eyes might determine who was waiting there and said, "Hello, Herman, what can I do for you?"

I had the feeling that the manager was forearmed with coolness just in case I might be wanting to open a new account to buy something on credit, which happily for me was not the case. When I explained that I had merely come by to speak, he seemed unable to comprehend such a wanton waste of time and seemed to mentally dismiss the whole affair as he nervously fingered the papers in his hand until I moved on to locate a more hospitable acquaintance.

Thus, I did not expect any more cordiality than I received when I advanced to speak to Mr. Billy, but was satisfied that in his undemonstrative but friendly way Mr. Billy seemed pleased to see me.

Rebel sniffed Mr. Billy's dog and the latter returned the canine courtesy as Mr. Billy and I chatted a bit about the length of time since we had last met. I doubted that Mr. Billy had any present recollection of when we last met, or how long it had been, or what might have been talked about, or what had transpired since that time. I asked about Miss Estelle and Cho Cho and Malcolm.

As we stood there and chatted, I realized that we were about one hundred yards from the great hickory tree where twenty-three years before I had almost been caught poaching Mr. Billy's squirrel, but this was no time for that sort of reminiscing. Indeed, there would never be such a time, and I put that recollection out of my mind. I recalled that in our last chat Mr. Billy had expressed some satisfaction over the fact that the filming of *Intruder in the Dust* was providing employment for many people of the town. This thought prompted an unexpected sequence of events.

Having known Mr. Billy to be the gently spoken story teller of childhood years, the philosopher of Hollywood, and the epitome of poise and bearing and easy grace, I was scarcely prepared for what was about to occur.

I remarked that I was out to run my bird dog a little and thought that I might find some interesting ground down the Old Taylor Road and that we also might get to see the new factory which had been built down the road a half mile or so.

Mr. Billy did not respond.

I said, "It seems like lots of progress is being made with this big new factory down there. I understand it is providing lots of jobs."

I looked off in the distance in the general direction of the new factory and became aware of a sound that I had never heard. It was something like a guttural growl or of muffled words. I turned to look at Mr. Billy and could scarcely believe my eyes. It seemed that sparks were leaping from Mr. Billy's eyes as his fury soared to an explosive level and his face went through contortions of emotion.

I was dumbfounded.

Finally Mr. Billy's hissing words became understandable, and I was even more astounded.

Mr. Billy said: "Here we have the most wonderful little town in the world and they are trying to change it into something like a damned mill town in Connecticut or North Carolina."

I fumbled for words and mumbled some unintelligible sound. Then I realized that I had unwittingly tripped the trigger of some pent-up frustration of Mr. Billy's. What could have been the source of his frustration? Perhaps it may have been like the ferment of the grape which builds up pressure until the cork is blown.

In condemning the impending changes, Mr. Billy's wrath appeared to have spent itself, as though he had reset his circuit breaker. His eyes returned to normal. He looked into the distance as he stuffed his pipe and a signaling pause ensued.

I could think of nothing else I wanted to say. Each of us seemed to understand that our brief reunion had ended.

Mr. Billy put his pipe in his mouth, drew his dog a little closer, pulled his hat down by the front brim, and extended his hand. I felt relieved in finding that it was not I who had so infuriated Mr. Billy. Rather it was "industrialization" about which Mr. Billy was upset. I eagerly shook Mr. Billy's hand and said, "Good to see you again, Mr. Billy."

Mr. Billy gestured his reciprocal feelings by lifting his pipe a little while slightly nodding his head. Then he turned unhurriedly and started strolling toward the entrance gate to his yard and the cedar-shaded driveway beyond.

I motioned to old Rebel to get into the car. I put my pipe in my mouth, then got in and started the engine in the almost thoughtless and habitual movements of one completely preoccupied. I finally shifted into the lower gear and eased the car forward until it topped the crest of the rise before reaching the city limits. There the pavement ended, and I became vaguely conscious of the sound of the gravel beginning to crunch beneath the tires. The car had coasted down the hill as I thoughtfully tried to comprehend the real meaning of Mr. Billy's disapproval of industrial development.

Was it the prospect of industrial progress which had aroused Mr. Billy's ire? Could it have been the threat of the Sartorisian and Snopesian establishment being replaced by people of different castes, such as Negroes, outlanders, foreigners, and Yankees working with capital and for unions controlled in far-off places? Were these threats to Jefferson and Yoknapatawpha as Mr. Billy had known them?

Were the town of Jefferson and the County of Yoknapatawpha mere fantasies which might vanish with the advent of economic change? Would the factory building on the horizon threaten Mr. Billy's sources of inspiration: of rivalries between deteriorating families in a post-Civil War society; of one-room wooden shacks heated by an open fire of sticks and brush in fireplaces which held a cooking pot, and where no inside plumbing had ever been; of outhouse privies and water drawn from wells or springs; of wages below the subsistance level, if wages could be had at all; of the population of eroded worn-out hillside fields; of Snopeses, Sartorises, and barnburners; of hamlets and country stores; of incest and miscegenation; of small fry merchant princes extracting what they could from even lower economic castes and of klansmen and lynch mobs who ruled by night?

Whether these stories were fashioned from fact or fiction in Mr. Billy's mind, the environment which stimulated them appeared to be destined for a pervasive change. Dream castles were crumbling in Yoknapatawpha.

I felt a little less enthusiastic about visiting the Chambers range plant than I had been before talking with Mr. Billy.

As I thought about the encounter later, I realized that several factors unbeknownst to me at the time of my meeting with Mr. Billy could have affected his response. An election had been scheduled in Oxford respecting the approval of a bond issue which would benefit the Chambers range plant. Perhaps this was what brought to the flashing point Mr. Billy's pent-up rage and incited his condemnation of the economic development he foresaw and detested.

There was to be a vote on the issue of municipal bonds to raise the funds for some capital improvement or utility services at the plant. The factory had proven to be an economic success in the community. The issue of the bonds enjoyed the support of most civic groups, including the Junior Chamber of Commerce. The election was only a few days away.

The existence of industry in Lafayette County was not new. That could hardly account for Mr. Billy's outrage over a bond issue for the improvement of the Chambers range plant.

About a half-mile to the west of Mr. Billy's home, through the University Woods, was Mill Street. As a youth living in the big red brick house on the Ole Miss campus, Mr. Billy would have overlooked the "industrial complex" along the railroad a quarter of a mile or so south from where he lived. There was a lumber mill, an ice plant, an oil mill, and, in the 1930s, a bottling plant. He knew these well. In his novel *Light in August,* he wrote of a lumber mill, probably having this one in mind, which provided employment for Joe Christmas, the bootlegger, murderer of a white woman, and victim of an overzealous deputy's bullets when he escaped. Joe had shoveled sawdust and rolled cigarettes at what presumably was this lumber mill in Mr. Billy's imagination. There were no others close to Oxford. The ice plant which once had been owned by Mr. Billy's father, provided a little stream of water which the Falkner boys dammed up to make a swimming hole, according to Johncy Falkner's book *My Brother Bill.*

The bottling plant was owned by Mr. Billy's father-in-law, Major Lemuel Early Oldham, during its brief existence in the early 1930s when the Major was trying to earn a livelihood in business after many years on the federal payroll. For many years these were Oxford's principal claims to manufacturing industries, but they had fallen into disuse and decay or been destroyed by fire. The lumber mill and oil mill burned in the middle 1920s. Barrels of oil exploded and threw other barrels about a hundred feet in the air as I had watched.

The Nehi bottling plant also was unsuccessful. The remains of these once busy plants, along with what had been a concrete swimming pool, were abandoned. A few minute's stroll along the trail in front of Mr. Billy's house and through the University Woods would take the walker along the trail to the former industrial site. A swimming hole along the trail appears to be described in Mr. Billy's early novel entitled *Soldier's Pay*. Thus, I reasoned, it was not just the presence of industry in the county which had upset Mr. Billy.

Then could it be the threat of increased taxes upon his property, which would be occasioned by the bond issue for the benefit of the Chambers range factory?

So far as I knew, Mr. Billy owned no substantial amount of property in Oxford which would be subject to taxation other than his home. His home in Bailey's Woods was within the city limits and consisted of about fourteen acres, more or less. While it was subject to both city and county taxes, this seemed an unlikely reason for Mr. Billy to be distraught over the possibility that his taxes might be increased by burdensome proportions. That probably was not the reason.

Could there be some violation of Mr. Billy's philosophy and principles of political economics? Republican philosophy appeared to me to embrace the idea that business should pay its own way, that taxpayers' money should not subsidize a business, and that businesses which could not pay their way should disappear from the market place. It was true that Mr. Billy's father-in-law, Major Oldham, had been "Mr. Republican" in Mississippi for a time, but that had been about a quarter of a century earlier. Doubtless Mr. Billy had absorbed some of the Major's thinking while he was still alive. This fell short, in my view, of supplying the causation for Mr. Billy's opposition to the bond issue to be so strong that it was the cause of his little tantrum.

Suppose, I said to myself, that Mr. Billy be taken at his word to the effect that they are trying to change this most wonderful town in the world into something like "a damned mill town in Connecticut or North Carolina."

Mr. Billy was well acquainted with the environment of Oxford and Lafayette County, including political, legal, social, and economic aspects. The last of these, the economic, may have been the most important to those who lived there. In the period in which Mr. Billy had grown up, there were intervals when the local economy was less depressed than usual. Usually it was something like a postslavery era, wherein jobs, if available at all, might provide insufficient income for the necessities, much less for reasonable comfort. In the 1930s, wages of fifty cents or a dollar per day were often hard to get. This was before there was such a thing as a "minimum wage." More frequently, jobs were not available.

It was a time when small boys delivered papers for a few cents a day. In the mid-1930s, I worked for a chain grocery store in the afternoon and on Saturday at a compensation of six dollars per week. On Saturday a work day usually started about 7:00 A.M. and lasted for eighteen hours until after midnight. Even so, my job was better than most teenage boys could get in Oxford.

Mr. Billy grew up in this environment. Stories in Oxford are plentiful as to some of his employment experiences. He reportedly painted the steeply sloping roof of Ventress Hall, formerly the library and law school building, of the university. He shoveled coal at the university power plant. He got a job at a bank in Oxford but kept it for only a short time. He served for several years as the postmaster for the university.

I pursued this line of thinking. Was the environment of Oxford and Lafayette County so good that Mr. Billy did not want it changed? How could one factory in Oxford make it like the mill towns in Connecticut and North Carolina? Those are the things Mr. Billy had mentioned. What was it that he valued in a community so beset with economic woes, particularly in the matter of jobs and opportunity? Did he cherish the stratified racial and social castes? Did he consider himself to be a member of the upper social tier? Was he of the Snopesian or Sartorisian class? Was he the champion of either of these? Together these disparate groups provided the raw material which had inspired his writings. The social structure had long resisted change. Although the social structure, like princes and castles, was interesting to write about, it was beginning to disintegrate.

Change had come to Yoknapatawpha and was increasing.

Within a few months of my chance encounter with Mr. Billy on the Old Taylor Road, he would be working on his novel entitled *The Town*. It was written between November 1955 and September 1956, and would be followed in 1959 by *The Mansion*. These novels picked up and continued the saga of the Snopes families which he had described many years before in 1940 in *The Hamlet*.

The Snopeses in his later novels were depicted by Mr. Billy in their decline after a period of escalating good fortune which had carried Flem Snopes, the son of a migrant sharecropper farmer, to the presidency of the bank and closer to the attainment of his aspiration for "respectability."

Eula Varner Snopes, the adulterous wife of Flem Snopes, committed suicide. Her illicit lover left town after being ousted as president of the bank by her husband. Flem Snopes was murdered by his cousin, Mink Snopes, who had been aided in committing the murder by Linda Snopes and her lawyer. Linda was the legal, but not the actual, daughter of Flem. Flem had spared her illegitimacy by marrying the pregnant Eula before Linda was born. The Snopesian period of ascendency was ended for many of Mr. Billy's principal characters by their own deeds or the deed of a relative or friend, as if a curse were on their kind and those who came too close to them.

I guessed that Mr. Billy was showing the ephemeral nature of success and the difficulties of improving the status of the class into which one is born; that temporarily one may succeed in climbing upward in "respectability," but may encounter obstacles in staying there; and that one may be brought back down by one's own kind to the level of the caste which creates a person.

The Sartoris clan and members of their class, who fancied themselves as descendants of the "cotton aristocracy" of the upper classes of the Atlantic colonies or of Europe, had problems of their own. They fared little better, if better at all, than the Snopeses. Through suicidal recklessness in cars and planes and default in procreation, their number was steadily dwindling on the Jefferson scene. Few, outside of relatives and friends, were considered good enough to marry, and if they married within the prohibited degrees of kin, the family idiot might be their prize. If they married beneath the caste, they might be ostracized. In their small and shrinking communal society opportunities in selection of a mate were limited, and bachelors and old maids would not perpetuate their lines.

In trying to understand Mr. Billy's feelings, I began to connect such information as I could recall of things Mr. Billy had said, and I tried to discover his state of mind at the time the statements were made.

In 1950 in Stockholm, in accepting the Nobel Prize for literature, Mr. Billy had expressed the belief that man not only would endure but that he would also prevail. To me this had a positive and hopeful overtone. Had Mr. Billy's optimism of 1950 changed to pessimism by 1955 when I had talked with him?

I then remembered that in March 1959, Mr. Billy completed the writing of *The Mansion,* which appeared to illustrate the futility of trying to gain "respectability." Respectability had eluded Flem Snopes, who had tried to build it upon opportunism, deceit, and trickery, instead of earning respectability by doing good. His own murder by his kinsman Mink Snopes was his reward.

I conceded to myself that Mr. Billy's ambivalance was hard to figure out. Did Mr. Billy really want to preserve the environment from which came the Snopes and Sartoris classes in Yoknapatawpha County? I began to wonder if there might have been some symbolic connection between Mr. Billy's outrage concerning the changes he foresaw in the coming of industrialization to his hometown and his dispositions by suicide and murder of the members of the Flem Snopes family in *The Town* and *The Mansion.* They, too, had invaded the town and displaced some of the previous establishment.

There were more questions than answers: Does the environment make people as they are, or is it the reverse that's true? Would a thousand years of breeding mutate the Snopesian genes? Might changes in the environment reduce the grandeur of Sartorisian dreams? Might factory wages and unions and federal law and the right to vote by a growing population bring blacks or outsiders to political power?

What caused the Indians to lose lands they had held since pre-historic times, and thus to lose their way of life? Did their military, political, and economic weaknesses result from failure to adapt to educational, agricultural, and technological changes? Did these failings foretell the loss of their domain and genocidal banishment to reservations beyond a Trail of Tears? Could similar failings eventually displace the social order as Mr. Billy had known it?

Might prolonged adherence to the ways of the Old South, with agriculture as its economic base, bring decline to those who disdained industrialization and sought to perpetuate an outmoded social and political order?

Could the town and county remain the same while all the world was changing?

The election of 1955 was held concerning the bond issue for the Chambers plant improvements. When the votes were counted there was overwhelming support for the bond issue. The vote was something like three thousand for and around a dozen against the issue. It seemed to me that it might be possible to account for the few votes opposing the bond issue by counting the members of Mr. Billy's family and his closest relatives.

Had Mr. Billy's interests begun to differ from those of most of the people of Yoknapatawpha County and Jefferson?

Chapter 12

Retrospection

Within a quarter of a century after Mr. Billy's death in 1962, the quaint little town of Oxford had undergone many changes and had evolved into a bustling little city. Its population had greatly increased, and its boundaries had been expanded. The industrialization which Mr. Billy had foreseen and detested in 1955 had transpired, and several factories had been established in or near the city.

The Civil Rights Revolution in America had gotten underway shortly after Mr. Billy's death. One of the most important breakthroughs in that revolution occurred on the campus of the University of Mississippi in 1962 as James Meredith, a Negro, was forceably enrolled as a student in that university after a riot was quelled by federal troops. The Civil Rights Act of 1964 brought "Freedom Riders" into Mississippi to encourage Negroes to register and vote. Three of the "Riders" were murdered at Philadelphia, Mississippi, but the right of Negroes to vote was established, and the power of the Negro vote became manifest. By the 1980s Negroes had been elected or appointed to political positions at many levels including sheriffs, mayors, judges, members of the Supreme Court of Mississippi, U.S. Congressmen, and state legislators. Mississippians had elected two Republicans to serve in the U.S. Senate. The Republican Party had become the party of many whites, although Democrats continued to be elected to the U.S. House of Representatives and to state and local offices.

No longer did Negroes live in shanties on unpaved streets and roads near Birney's Branch or in "Freedman Town" or on the outskirts of Oxford. Instead they lived in well-built homes on paved streets. Sometimes they lived in previously all-white neighborhoods. Their children attended the public schools and the university without fear of interference or molestation.

Oxford and Lafayette County, as well as the rest of Mississippi and the entire South, had entered the post-Faulkner Era.

By the 1980s, many, if not most, of the people who may have inspired Mr. Billy's writing had passed from the Oxford scene. Some of the landmarks of Oxford and Lafayette County which may have been portrayed by Mr. Billy in fictional Jefferson and Yoknapatawpha County had been demolished and replaced. Yet, others remained and had been preserved, restored, or improved upon.

I tried to think of those people, events, and landmarks which may have influenced Mr. Billy's life or writings and which of them should be included in the lasting residue of the Faulkner Era. Among the most profound influences upon Mr. Billy had been the Oldham family and its home. The Oldham home on South Lamar Boulevard, where I had witnessed the reunion of Mr. Billy and Miss Estelle in 1924, with its manicured lawn and flower gardens, had fallen into decadence. After 1932, when Democrats came to power, Major Oldham's fortunes drastically declined from an affluent and powerful political position as U.S. attorney during Republican administrations. The Major unsuccessfully attempted the private practice of law. His business venture into the Nehi bottling plant also failed. The effects of the Depression were severe. He became poverty-stricken and remained so until his death in 1945.

The pitiable circumstances of the grand old house becoming a community eyesore seemed almost inconceivable to me. Finally the property was sold to the South Central Bell Telephone Company for its central office location, and the house was torn down. This debacle told the story of the fall of a political "house of cards." It represented the ultimate fate of a once-powerful Republican in

The Falkner Obelisk
In St. Peter's Cemetery in Oxford, a white marble obelisk stands at the graves of John Wesley Thompson Falkner, and Sallie Murry Falkner, the grandparents of William Faulkner. Beneath a stone likeness of Sallie Falkner on the obelisk is inscribed "Her children arise and call her blessed." In *The Town*, Faulkner describes a similar obelisk at the grave of Eula Snopes with the inscription "A virtuous wife is a crown to her husband. Her children rise and call her blessed."

Oxford during the ascendency of Democrats under Franklin D. Roosevelt.

It seemed to me that Mr. Billy's grandfather, John Wesley Thompson Falkner, one-time bank president and lawyer, had also greatly influenced Mr. Billy. His grandfather had owned what the Falkners called the Big Place, the large three-story frame house on South Lamar Boulevard.

The Big Place, had been moved in the late 1920s from its original position facing South Lamar Boulevard to the northwest corner of the lot where it faced University Avenue. It had for about fifty years served as rental property and had greatly depreciated in appearance. By the 1980s the house had been demolished and replaced by a food service business.

Mr. Billy's grandfather seems to have continued, even after his death, to influence Mr. Billy's thoughts. In St. Peter's Cemetery in Oxford there stands a white marble obelisk, about twenty or more feet high. Its square shaft gradually tapers to a pyramidal point. It marks the grave of John Wesley Thompson Falkner, the so-called "Young Colonel" who was Mr. Billy's grandfather. It is inside an iron fence which surrounds the plot where his wife and some of his children and their spouses and children are buried. Mr. Billy and his family are buried in his own cemetery lot a short distance to the northwest of the obelisk.

On the shaft of the obelisk about midway to the top is a stone likeness of the heads of Mr. Billy's grandfather on the north side and of his grandmother, Sallie Murry Falkner, on the south side, which are carved out of a darker stone. They are oval in shape. It

Photos courtesy of Herman E. Taylor

Stone Medallions
The stone medallions on the Falkner obelisk show the likenesses of John Wesley Thompson Falkner and Sallie Murry Falkner.

194

seemed to me that these stone carvings on the marble shaft may be what inspired Mr. Billy to describe a monument with a similar "medallion" carved out of stone, which, in *The Town*, was placed at the grave of Eula Varner Snopes, the adulterous and suicidal wife of Flem Snopes.

It could, however, have been inspired by the monument at the grave of Bem Price. To the south, about fifty yards or so, stands another similar obelisk with a stone medallion depicting Bem Price. He had once been the president of the Bank of Oxford. Jimmy Falkner told me that his great-grandfather and Bem Price had an understanding to the effect that the survivor of the two of them would have such an obelisk which would be six inches taller than that of the one who predeceased the other. Jimmy's great-grandfather did survive Bem Price, who had lived in the brick mansion on North Lamar Boulevard called Ammadelle, the most palatial home in Oxford.

The names *Bem* and *Flem* may, in Mr. Billy's imagination, have had some relationship. Bem Price was the president of a bank as Flem was the fictional president of a bank. Bem Price actually lived in a mansion and Flem's crowning achievement was the building of the mansion depicted by Mr. Billy in *The Mansion*. Bem actually had a medallion placed upon his obelisk while Flem in Mr. Billy's story had a similar medallion placed upon the monument at his wife's grave.

Dr. Evans Harrington, for many years the Director of the Faulkner and Yoknapatawpha Conference at the University of Mississippi, discounts the possibility of Bem Price stimulating Faulkner's imagination to create fictional Flem Snopes. Dr. Harrington stated his belief as follows:

> While Bem Price's first name may well have helped Faulkner settle on Flem for Snopes' first name, none of the rest of your discussion of Price makes a strong case for his having been, or suggested, the model for Flem. A very large argument against him for such a model is that he was from an old, moneyed family in the area, wasn't he? And his being a president of Faulkner's grandfather's rival bank, rather than a poor sharecropper's son, who ousted

Faulkner's grandfather to become president of the grand-
father's bank, makes him less a candidate for the model of
Flem than Joe Parks, who, though not a sharecropper, *was* a
shrewd trader from the Etta (Snopes) area, who *did* oust
Faulkner's grandfather and take over the grandfather's bank.
Moreover, Parks bought Murry Falkner's home after he re-
placed Faulkner's grandfather as bank president and later
Faulkner bought Park's old farm, Greenfield.*

The Thompson-Chandler house, facing South 13th Street (Lake
Street) is still standing in 1990, and it looks as it has since my early
childhood in the 1920s. The property suffered in its historical
value when some owner removed and sold the cast iron fence
which bordered the South 13th Street frontage. That iron fence
had once surrounded the Lafayette County Courthouse.

It had been along the cast iron fence where Mr. Billy had observed the plight of Edwin Chandler, who suffered from mental
disorder, that Mr. Billy became inspired to write of his fictional
character Benji in *The Sound and the Fury,* according to Johncy
Falkner's account in *My Brother Bill.*

The city water tank, which had stood east of the square behind
the J. E. Neilson Department Store, was one of the most obvious
landmarks in Oxford as Mr. Billy wrote of Jefferson. A similar water
tank was described in *The Town* and was where Flem Snopes, or
his confederates, or someone undetermined, hid the brass stolen
from the municipal power plant. I noted that the old tank had been
removed, and a new tank had been built near the Community
House on South 15th Street.

A home which has endured for more than a century was near
the north end of North Lamar Boulevard. Ammadelle, which has
been previously described, stands as a lasting monument to the
pre-Civil War affluence of the "landed aristocracy" of the South.
Built of brick and masonry, it was styled along the lines of an Ital-
ian villa in Tuscany, according to Jack Case Wilson's *Faulkners,
Fortunes and Flames.* It was begun in 1856 and completed after

*This was included in a letter from Dr. Evans Harrington dated May 22, 1989, to the author.

the Civil War for the Thomas Pegues family. A succession of well-to-do owners have periodically restored and modernized the house and maintained the gardens and grounds. This house appears likely to be one of the most lasting of Oxford's landmark homes.

The railroad had also been a prominent landmark on the Oxford (Jefferson) scene, particularly in the 1920s and early 1930s, but by the late 1930s it had lost much of its passenger haul to the automobile. By the 1960s the railroad's freight haul had also dwindled as trucks increasingly carried the freight. In the 1980s the rails and crossties were removed from a point which is about a mile south of Oxford near the "stove factory" to Coffeeville, Mississippi, about thirty-five miles to the south.

Mr. Billy, in his novels from *Soldier's Pay* in 1926 to *The Town* in 1956, described travel on this railroad. The railroad was an important factor in his novels as lover or seducer or villain or killer left Jefferson by train and thereby made a permanent exit from his stories.

As late as 1959 in *The Mansion,* Mr. Billy described how the murderer Mink Snopes had followed the railroad tracks on foot into Jefferson for the purpose of killing his cousin Flem Snopes. The railroad, by the end of Mr. Billy's life in 1962, had lost its place, except for the heaviest freight, as the principal means of transportation into and away from Oxford.

The Lafayette County Jail, which probably inspired Mr. Billy's description of the Yoknapatawpha County Jail, has been torn down and replaced by a modern structure. No longer does the jailer's family live in the downstairs portion of the jail beneath the prisoners on the upper level.

By the 1980s the Lafayette County Courthouse had been renovated and enlarged. New wings had been built on both east and west sides. Mr. Billy had forestalled its demolition in earlier years by articles in *The Oxford Eagle* praising its architecture and had romanticized the history of the courthouse and the jail in *Requiem For a Nun* in 1951.

Perhaps the courthouse is the most impressive Oxford landmark which has survived. The courthouse was built between 1836 and

1840, partially destroyed by Yankee troops in 1864, rebuilt in 1872, expanded in 1952, and renovated and modernized in about 1980. It seems to me to be a lasting monument to Mr. Billy, who helped prevent its demolition and encouraged its preservation and improvement. A plaque at the south door of the courthouse contains a quotation from *Requiem for a Nun.*

On the campus of the university where Mr. Billy had lived and worked in the 1920s, great changes had transpired in the intervening years. The university had grown in enrollment tenfold or more. Many of the faculty homes and buildings had been replaced and in some cases the replacement had later also been replaced.

The red brick house on the ridge near the University Avenue entrance to the university campus, which had been the home of Mr. Billy's parents in the 1920s, later became the Delta Psi Fraternity House, then was replaced in 1950 by the Alumni House of the university. It had been surrounded by landmarks depicted in *Sanctuary* and other Faulkner novels.

The post office where Mr. Billy had worked had been replaced by the Pharmacy Building. The power plant, where he had shoveled coal in 1929 is still standing, but the great brick smokestack had been demolished by the mid-1980s.

Some "landmarks" remain much the same as when Mr. Billy lived nearby in the 1920s. The Lyceum, built in the 1840s, with its six massive concrete columns on both the east and the west ends, had been preserved and modernized and still serves as the administrative office building. The Lyceum and the "old chapel," later the Y.M.C.A. Building, are said to have served as hospitals for Confederate soldiers after the Battle of Shiloh and also as hospitals for Yankee wounded at other times.

Ventress Hall, built in 1889, is near the Confederate Monument on the campus and close to the center of the Grove. Resembling the house in which the Falkners had lived on the campus, it was built of red brick and is of Gothic architectural design. Mr. Billy is said to have painted the steeply sloping roof of its turret when other painters declined to take the risk involved.

The Student Union building was built on the former site of the Coop, as the girls' dormitories, Ricks and Ward halls, were called

Mr. Billy's Riding Trail
In Bailey's Woods south of Rowan Oak, a trail runs west from Old Taylor Road. On June 17, 1962, William Faulkner took his last ride along this path. He was thrown from the horse and sustained injuries which led to his death on July 6, 1962.

and which were referred to in *Sanctuary* as where Temple Drake lived. The annual Faulkner and Yoknapatawpha Conference is held in the Student Union building. The seminar attracts Faulkner scholars from many parts of the world. It is held in the last week of July each year to study Mr. Billy's writings.

To the west of the Student Union building is Fulton Chapel, where Mr. Billy delivered his address to the graduating class of University High School in 1951. His daughter Jill was a member of that class. In Fulton Chapel on August 3, 1987, the regional postmaster general of the United States delivered an address and issued a postage stamp commemorating William Faulkner and bearing his picture on the stamp.

I recalled my last visit to Mr. Billy's home in Bailey's Woods. Among the best preserved Oxford landmarks of the period in

199

Rowan Oak After Renovation
William Faulkner purchased this house in 1930 for $6,000. He renovated it and lived here until his death in 1962.

which Mr. Billy wrote was that of his own home. His daughter Jill, after his death, transferred the property to the university. The university had restored and preserved the buildings and grounds to an appearance very much the way they were when Mr. Billy resided there. Rowan Oak is on a plateau of about four acres bounded by steeply sloping terrain on the east, north, and west. To the south the front yard gradually slopes to the front fence. Outside the fence is a short lane of perhaps two hundred yards which runs west from the Old Taylor Road and separates the lawn from the thick forest of about ten acres, to the south of the lane, which borders the Old Taylor Road. A trail through the University Woods runs west to the "new" Old Taylor Road for about a half mile.

Along this trail Mr. Billy took his last horseback ride a week or so before his death. On that ride he was thrown from his horse. He never fully recovered from the injuries he sustained. He had ridden over to the former site of an ice plant his father had once operated near the railroad.

Mr. Billy's homesite and Bailey's Woods to the south of it consisted of about fourteen acres. After Mr. Billy's death, my brother, Guy B., sold the university about eighteen acres of land to the north of the original Rowan Oak property, which had once been known as Brown's Pasture.

After Mr. Billy's death in 1962 and after Guy B. had acquired the Brown's Pasture property, a dispute arose concerning the boundary line between the Rowan Oak property and the pasture property. Guy B. was represented by W. P. ("Billy") Price, the husband of Katherine Sue, the daughter of Mr. Billy's Uncle John. The case went through lengthy litigation and finally was appealed to the Supreme Court of Mississippi where Guy B. won. The ultimate resolution of the controversy occurred when both properties were acquired by the University of Mississippi. When the university acquired both Rowan Oak and Brown's Pasture, some considered the pasture land to be a part of Rowan Oak. It is sometimes called the Faulkner Woods. That is why it is said that Rowan Oak includes thirty-two acres of land instead of the original fourteen.

Rowan Oak's cedar-bordered driveway, wide enough for a single vehicle, winds northwestwardly from the curve of the Old Taylor Road toward Mr. Billy's former home. A hundred yards or so along the drive stands, as of 1990, a white two-story frame house, covered with wood weather board siding. Each board overlapped a lower board, as did many, if not most frame houses built in Oxford in the period around 1844-1848.

On the front of the house are four white square-edged columns, rectangular in cross section, which ascend twenty feet or so. They taper from a width at the bottom of about eighteen inches to about twelve inches at their tops. They are made of solid wood and each appears to have been hewn from a single tree. They rise to support the roof which shelters the small porch. The porch is mounted by

William Faulkner's Magnolia Tree
This tree stands on the south lawn of Rowan Oak. The brickwork around the tree
was designed by the gardener of Jacob Thompson, who lived across Old Taylor
Road during the 1840s and 50s.

several brick steps leading up from the brick entrance walk which
runs from the unloading point at the driveway.

Nina Claire and I went inside the house with a tour group in
1982. I was greatly surprised when the tour guide and custodian of
the property, Dr. James W. Webb, an old friend of mine, brought
out a manuscript of a book. He said that it had been found underneath the stairway when the university took possession of the
property. What excited me was that this manuscript appeared to
be the one which Malcolm Franklin and I and our friends had examined in the house in 1930, when we had also experimented
with smoking Mr. Billy's cigarettes.

On the table in the west room was the old Underwood typewriter looking as it had more than a half-century before.

To the west the land levels out and extends to and beyond a
wooden picket fence which surrounds the vegetable garden. Farther to the west is level land where I played baseball in the early

1930s. Even when I was a boy, the wooden palings, which made up the fence, were showing signs of sag and rot and their blackish gray color revealed that they were very old when Mr. Billy purchased the property in 1930.

Midway between the house and the front fence is a great magnolia tree with a trunk about four feet in diameter. It has several limbs of massive size, perhaps two feet in thickness, extending out from the trunk. Around the tree is an elaborate pattern of concentric circles of brick terrace ascending and extending outward about fifteen feet from the trunk.

It was around the foot of this tree that the teenage contemporaries of mine sometimes stashed their half-pints of gin when Cho Cho gave a party. I was astonished to find that the scene around the magnolia tree was almost exactly as I recalled it having been when I was a boy. I was not surprised when one of my sons disclosed that in the 1970s, the terrace around that tree was a favorite place for Ole Miss students to gather to smoke pot.

As I left the magnolia tree, Nina Claire and I sauntered toward the fence along the lane to the south of the lawn to see if the large hickory tree, where once I had poached one of Mr. Billy's squirrels, might still be there.

I fell into a pensive mood as I recalled that most of those who were alive when I last walked this way were now dead, including Mr. Billy, Miss Estelle, Cho Cho, and Malcolm. Life, it seemed to me, was much too transient a state of being. I took some comfort from the appearance of agelessness of the magnolia tree. Then I felt some despair as I thought that even it, like all living things, in time must fall and return to dust.

I had heard that Malcolm Franklin had written a book entitled *Bitterweeds*. He had spent much of his life working as an assistant in the medical school of the University of Mississippi, moving to Jackson when the school was moved there. Malcolm died in 1977 and was buried in Mr. Billy's plot in St. Peter's Cemetery in Oxford.

Cho Cho was said to have returned to Shanghai where her father lived and to have remarried, thus becoming Mrs. William Fielden. At some point she returned to Oxford where she spent her last years. She died in Oxford in 1975.

Photo courtesy of Herman E. Taylor

Native Soil
In his native soil of Oxford and Lafayette County, Mr. Billy found eternal rest in St. Peter's Cemetery. He had envisioned this final resting place in "A Green Bough," written in 1919.

My old liver and white pointer bird dog named Rebel, who had been with me when I met Mr. Billy on the Old Taylor Road in 1955, had expired in his seventeenth year and was put to rest outside my study near a large holly tree in Memphis. In Rebel's place, my constant companion was a black and tan German Shepherd named Star—a Seeing Eye Dog acquired in 1977 because my vision had declined. After serving as my guide and protector for more than thirteen years, Star died March 17, 1990. She is buried next to Rebel beneath the holly tree.

I mused: Might it be possible that some of Mr. Billy's thoughts and writings would be more lasting than most living things or structures and landmarks of man's creation?

Mr. Billy clearly stated his views concerning the lasting importance of the writer and poet to the perpetuation of man.

In accepting the Nobel Prize for literature in 1950 in Stockholm, he said:

> I believe that man will not merely endure. He will prevail. He is immortal, not because he alone among creatures has an inexhaustible voice, but because he has a soul, a spirit capable of compassion and sacrifice and endurance.
>
> The poet's, the writer's, duty is to write about these things. It is his privilege to help man endure by lifting his heart, by reminding him of the courage and honor and hope and pride and compassion and pity and sacrifice which have been the glory of his past.
>
> The poet's voice need not merely be the record of man. It can be one of the props, the pillars, to help him endure and prevail.

I meditated upon these beliefs of Mr. Billy and was troubled by my inability to understand Mr. Billy's conclusion that man is "immortal" because he has a soul, a spirit capable of compassion and sacrifice and endurance. These questions came to my mind:

Just how long did Mr. Billy contemplate that man would endure? Over what did Mr. Billy believe man would prevail? How could such writing help man endure and prevail?

It occurred to me that no one could ever prove Mr. Billy's beliefs concerning man's ability to endure and prevail to be in error. If man should fail to endure, to whom might proof of Mr. Billy's errors be submitted?

Had Mr. Billy contemplated this bar to refutation of what has become the most widely quoted, and possibly the most lasting, of his philosophies?

When I approached the fence along the lane my heart pounded with excitement for, despite my poor vision, I saw the big limb of the hickory tree extending about fifty feet from the north side of the trunk. The tree appeared as I recalled it looking when I had last seen it in 1933.

As I stood there entranced in reverie and watching the movement of the leaves in the gentle breeze. The breeze suddenly grew stronger and the great limb lifted upward, then moved downward as if bowing in recognition of an old acquaintance, one whose ramblings would forever lead back to my own and Faulkner's Oxford.

Acknowledgments

The writing of this book was inspired by the author's esteemed friend and former instructor, Dr. Adwin Wigfall Green, professor of English at the University of Mississippi. Soon after William Faulkner's death in 1962, Dr. Green requested the author's recollections of William Faulkner for inclusion in a book which he was preparing. Circumstances prevented the author's compliance with this request in time for it to be included in that book, which was entitled *William Faulkner of Mississippi.*

The author also acknowledges the help he received from his close friend, Colonel Robert M. Cook, U.S. Army Retired, in reviewing the manuscript and advising as to its contents.

The contribution of Francis S. Bowling, retired associate justice of the Supreme Court of Mississippi, in providing historical information, is greatly appreciated.

The QUIC reference service of the Memphis Public Library, Memphis, Tennessee, has provided essential research and information.

Sharron Eve Sarthou, senior library assistant of the University of Mississippi, has provided much historical information.

Elisabeth Stephens Rounsaville, the owner of the Stephens-Ragland log house which appears in chapter 8, "Roads," provided much valuable historical information concerning this property.

The typing by Josephine Nabors Horsley and the patient reading and correction by Dorothy Childers Boyd were indispensable to the completion of the book. The competent proofreading and correction of the manuscript by Lynn Coates and Reletha Upton were also greatly appreciated.

The author is especially grateful to Mr. and Mrs. William Henry Tate of Oxford, Mississippi, for providing a photograph of the former Henry L. Tate home on Johnson Avenue (Lake Street) which appears in chapter 9, "Rambling."

Mr. William Lewis, Jr., of the J. E. Neilson Company of Oxford, Mississippi, provided the photograph of the Lafayette County Courthouse in 1908 that appears in the first chapter.

Mrs. Martha Stephens Cofield and Mr. Jack Cofield of Cofield's Studio in Oxford, Mississippi, provided many of the other photographs.

Mrs. Pamela Prather Coll of the word processing department of Memphis State University provided indispensable services in reproducing the material in *Faulkner's Oxford.*

The author proudly acknowledges the aid of his daughter, Claire Taylor Dickerson, in reviewing and editing this book. She is the author of the last seventeen words.

—Herman E. Taylor

Bibliography

Blotner, Joseph. *Faulkner: A Biography.* 1 vol. ed. New York: Random House, 1984.

Cowley, Malcolm. *The Portable Faulkner.* Rev. and ex. ed. New York: Viking Press, Inc., 1946.

Faulkner, Jim. *Across the Creek.* Jackson: University Press of Mississippi, 1986.

Faulkner, John. *My Brother Bill: An Affectionate Reminiscence.* New York: Trident Press, 1963.

Faulkner, William. *Absalom, Absalom.* New York: Random House, 1936; New York: Modern Library, 1951; New York: Vintage, 1972.

————. *Intruder in the Dust.* New York: Random House, 1948; New York: Modern Library, 1964; New York: Vintage, 1972.

————. *Light in August.* New York: Harrison Smith and Robert Haas, 1932; New York: Random House, 1967; New York: Vintage 1972.

————. *The Reivers.* New York: Random House, 1962; New York: Vintage, 1966.

————. *Requiem for a Nun.* 3rd printing. New York: Random House, 1951; New York: Vintage, 1975.

————. *Sanctuary.* New York: Random House, 1962; New York: Modern Library, 1964; New York: Vintage, 1963.

————. *Sartoris.* New York: Harcourt, Brace, 1929; New York: Random House, 1956.

————. *Soldiers' Pay.* New York: Boni and Liveright, 1926; New York: Liveright, 1951.

————. *The Hamlet.* 3rd ed. New York: Random House, 1954.

————. *The Mansion.* New York: Random House, 1959; New York: Vintage, 1965.

————. *The Town.* New York: Vintage, 1961.

Lowry, Robert and William S. McCardle. *A History of Mississippi.* New Orleans and New York: University Publishing Company, 1893.

The Oxford Eagle, Oxford, Mississippi.

Runyan, Harry. *The Faulkner Glossary.* Secaucus, New Jersey: Citadel Press, 1964.

The Skipwith Historical and Genealogical Society, Inc. *The Heritage of Lafayette County Mississippi.* Dallas: Curtis Media Corporation, 1986.

Wade, James M. and A. W. Green. *William Faulkner of Mississippi.* Baton Rouge, Louisiana: State University Press, 1965.

Wilson, Jack. *Faulkners, Fortunes and Flames.* Nashville: Annadale Press, 1984.

About the Author

Herman Eugene Taylor was born December 2, 1918, in Oxford, Mississippi. He is the youngest son of Guy B. and Kate Stephens Taylor. He is the great-great-great-grandson of Captain Daniel Taylor (1748-1826) who served in the Continental Army from North Carolina during the Revolutionary War. Daniel Taylor moved to what became Carroll County, Mississippi, where he lived until his death in 1826. The author is the great-great-grandson of Dr. John Taylor (1787-1865) who founded Taylor, Mississippi, as mentioned in chapter 7.

Herman E. Taylor graduated from the University of Mississippi in 1940 and received a commission as a second lieutenant in the U.S. Army Reserve from that University. He entered active duty on October 10, 1940, and served in the Sixth Infantry Division and X Corps during World War II in the New Guinea and Philippine campaigns, including the invasion of Leyte and Mindanao. He attained the rank of major during World War II and received the Bronze Star for meritorius service.

He served as Advisor for Veterans and Supervisor of Housing at the University of Mississippi from 1946 to 1950. He graduated from the law school at Ole Miss in 1951 and was immediately recalled to active duty in the army during the Korean Conflict. He served until October 1954, attaining the rank of lieutenant colonel.

In 1955, Taylor received the degree of master of laws from New York University. He entered law practice in Memphis, Tennessee, in 1956 and served on the faculty of Memphis State University until 1988 as professor of business law. He now holds the title of professor emeritus.

He is also the author of many professional articles, including "The Doctoral Restoration in Legal Education" published in 1972 in the *Tennessee Bar Journal.* This article helped establish the degree of doctor of jurisprudence, the juris doctor degree, as the professional degree in law in all accredited law schools in the United States.

Taylor is married to the former Nina Claire Gates of Clarksdale, Mississippi, and they have five children and nine grandchildren. Herman Eugene Taylor, Jr., is an investment banker in Little Rock, Arkansas. Glenn Gates Taylor and Claire Taylor Dickerson are lawyers practicing in Jackson, Mississippi. Dr. Stephens Davis Taylor, is a general surgeon in Huntsville, Alabama, and William McLarty Jarratt Taylor is an investment banker in Memphis, Tennessee.

Taylor Farm, a tree farm of about 270 acres on Clear Creek Road a few miles west of Taylor, Mississippi, is a frequent gathering place of the Taylor family. From its high hills one can see for many miles across the valley of the Yocona River, whose Chickasaw name, *Yocona Petopha,* became one of the world's most famous fictional places, Yoknapatawpha County.